Changing Conversations for a

CHANGING W🦠RLD

VOLUME TWO

How COVID-19 Changed
the Future of Work:
Aspirations, Opportunities,
Best Practices

Compiled by the European C-IQ Collective

Dedication

This book is an homage to all the innovative, courageous, and resilient people who are surviving and adapting in a changing world

Changing Conversations for a

CHANGING W🦠RLD

VOLUME TWO

How COVID-19 Changed the Future of Work: Aspirations, Opportunities, Best Practices

Compiled by the European C-IQ Collective

the three
tomatoes

The Three Tomatoes Publishing

CONTENTS

Introduction

By Tanja Murphy-Ilibasic
Chairwoman of the European C-IQ Collective

In August 2020, the European C-IQ (Conversational Intelligence®) Collective published the first volume of *Changing Conversations for a Changing World*, capturing a multitude of perspectives from professional coaches who all shared a common foundation in Judith E. Glaser's Conversational Intelligence®. At the time of publication, the COVID-19 pandemic had brought the world as we know it to a complete halt. And yet, few had anticipated that it would continue to define our values, interactions, and very existence at the most profound level.

The initial feelings of being overwhelmed and the helplessness felt by many at the beginning of the crisis have given way to the heaviness of oversaturation. This is strongly being driven by the plethora of tools and technologies, techniques, and practices that have arisen to support our efforts to adapt to the erratic, ever-shifting challenges we face. The question is how to navigate these rocky shores, beckoning with alluring attractions whilst hiding the fundamental needs of both technical and facilitative expertise in the depths. How do we judge when enough is enough or whether we have even recognised what our needs are?

A first step is to internalise that people and organisations are unique, as are their requirements. They may share similarities and feel interchangeable at moments, yet a closer look will expose distinguishing features, cultures, and desires. This uniqueness demands an acceptance that solutions of worth are finely tailored garments, precisely fitted to a given individual, team, organisation, or circumstance. It demands an acceptance that organisational change does not occur overnight and that any changes themselves may have to pivot to a constantly shifting environment. It demands that we recognise not only our challenges but also the empowerment within our grasp.

Identifying what we share and value above all else unites us. The inherent desire for acceptance, trust, and inter-connectedness is within us all. It builds the unassailable foundation upon which healthy communities are built, enabling them to not only withstand the pressures of external forces but to thrive under their assault. It allows for inspirational energy to emerge and for individuals to shine brighter than ever before. It changes cultures and the concept of powerful leadership.

Very similar to Volume 1, this book is a collection of vantage points, of experiences and insights. It presents differentiated engagements in the form of case studies, exploration of values, and personal growth. The chapters are as diverse as the authors and the circumstances they depict. They are examples of understanding and adapting to unique needs. Perhaps they inspire you to consider how you could support the uniqueness that is your organisation or team. We hope so.

We are the European C-IQ Collective.

1
Taking My Own Medicine: A Personal Case History on the Change Curve

by Catharina Wöhlecke-Haglund
Leadership Trainer | Coach | Change Facilitator
Stockholm, Sweden

"Join me on a journey through the 'Change Curve,' when 2020 took us all online and out of our comfort zone."

In early 2020, coming home from a ski trip to France, I reflected on how happy I was with where I had come in my professional and personal life. As a coach, trainer, facilitator of change processes, and leadership in organizations, I had, of course, been taking my own medicine in setting goals and making myself an attractive vision for the last five years of my working life. And now it was here—the dream had become a reality.

I had engagements with global companies such as Molnlycke Healthcare in a talent program with a great colleague, Patrick Stahl. I had ongoing leadership programs with If Insurance on a Nordic level with another inspiring partner, Mikael Larsson. My friend and colleague Catarina Kentell and I were planning to write a book about feedback that we find missing on the market. Moa Diseborn and I continued to develop courses for project leaders on the leadership part of that profession. A kickstart program for leadership teams was on the drawing board with Ursula Nyqvist and Hanna Hedberg—and on top of that, a few other contracts were upcoming. The great, inspiring group of colleagues in The European Conversational Intelligence Collective who we were going to meet in Scotland in the fall to have fun with and learn together.

On a private note, I had the next ski trip to Svalbard booked, a trip to New York where I once lived was planned, and a challenging and fun European Senior Golf Association Tournament in Prague was something to look forward to. The kids had jobs or studies that were going fine, and we traveled together. I had it all planned to perfection. What more could you wish for?

If you have not worked with the Change Curve or the Kubler Ross Curve, here it is. It is a curve that most people in change go through. It can take a longer or shorter time, the phases can look a bit different, but in all, this is how we travel through change.

I am telling you about my journey because I think that you may be able to recognize it in yourself or others you meet. Hopefully, you can support them a little more or help yourself go through your curve faster now or at a subsequent time.

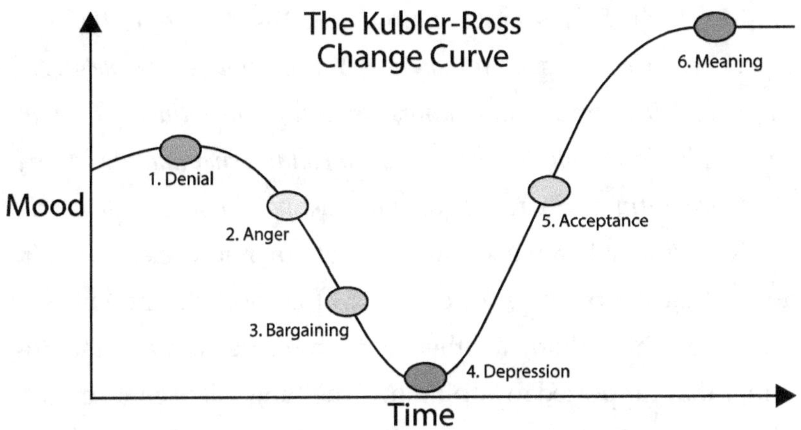

1. The Denial (and/or Shock): March

In March, we learned that the virus had come to Scandinavia, mainly through skiers on spring break in the alps. Some clients started to postpone the workshops and modules planned. Several courses were postponed and rescheduled forward a month or so (little did we know).

Me: *This will be over by summer. It can't be that bad, and there is no way this can last. So, I will wait a while and enjoy the time off.*

Like we do in denial, I chose to talk to others who said the same, agreed, and created their own "truth" about this situation. This will pass before we know it.

2. Anger (and/or Frustration): April

Things were not getting any better, and the postponing continued and got worse; now, people could not even be in their offices, let alone go to conferences and meeting places. A few clients talked about whether the training and activities could change into an online format.

Me: *It's not the same to meet online. You do not get the same experience. There is such a distance. You cannot see people's body language. There are so many things you cannot do online that we can do in a physical room. People have such bad internet and are so tired of online meetings. How am I going to make a living now? I hate this!*

Knowing what we know now about neuroscience, we're aware that the brain produces a lot of cortisol during stressful times. So, while talking to others with the same view and reading things that supported my opinion, something called confirmation bias took place. This mindset and way of thinking did not help to invite new perspectives or new learnings into my situation at all. On the contrary, my actions and viewpoint closed my ears and eyes to what could help me get on to a better place.

3. Bargaining: April

Still hoping that this would be over by summer, I could not think or do much with any sense of creativity and innovation. Some of my colleagues were trying to get me on board the idea of doing some excellent work in the digital format. Some of them did not give up, and for that, I am thankful today. This experience helped teach me not to give up on others when I lead change in any capacity.

Me: *Yes, but… Yes, but… Yes, but…*

4. Depression: May

Realizing that this would not pass very soon, I was hearing voices telling me this would be the case for the rest of the year, maybe longer. At this point, I had clients who have already decided to work from home for the rest of the year.

Me: *Oh, no—this is terrible.*

I was beginning to worry about my income and started looking into what support our government could give small businesses…not at all what I had thought of when we wished ourselves Happy New Year a few months back. Finally, I was forced to realize that there would be no trip to Scotland with my wonderful C-IQ European Collective Colleagues, nor any other trips for that matter.

Me: *How will I manage this? Maybe I am too old for this. Why do things like this happen to me? There is no solution. This new way of working feels impossible.*

5. Acceptance: June

I am thinking of one of the great tips from my master coach Maria Nemeth from Academy for Coaching Excellence: Find your vision, what is important to you, and make that clear! Then, it is all about following three basic steps:

1. Take baby steps
2. Get support
3. Celebrate success

And finally, you must realize that your Monkey Mind conversations will take you nowhere (you can read some of them in steps 2 through 4—and there are many more). The kind of thoughts that are about why it will not work, why it is hard or impossible, why I am impossible, or how this is not fair. After I understood how nonproductive such thoughts were, I started to be able to shift from those to more interesting conclusions.

Me: *This might be fun. I can do this. I want to be innovative.*

The first step with my colleague Catarina Kentell was to build a workshop about working online and what to think about when facing this new way of designing meetings. What better way to learn than to teach others? Today, we laugh about the part in the workshop that involved helping people find the chat box, the microphone, and the mute button. It has been a quick learning curve for us all, and we are now in a whole new place.

I took some more baby steps in changing my work habits with my dear partner, Patric Stahl, who is always first to play with tech tools and cool things. Among other things, he has fourteen barbecues for different cooking adventures—just saying!

We designed modules online step by step, testing tools over a beer, having an after work online with fun "props," inviting friends to be guinea pigs, and letting creativity flow. Was it perfect? No, but it took us a long way. You can read about some of the tools we harnessed at the end of this chapter.

6. Meaning: July and Forward

The whole meaning of online work had been reframed— from something hard and different to something without boundaries, where the sky's the limit.

The C-IQ European Collective took the next step. Instead of crying about not going to Scotland, we started on a new journey and a joint project. We said to each other: Let's build an online event in which we invite clients to share and learn with us about *Changing Conversations for a Changing World* (the first book, available on Amazon, by the way).

Karin Ovari introduced the Howspace learning platform, which I had seen before but never understood to its full potential. She deserves a lot of credit for inspiring others through the Change Curve with patience and perseverance.

Me: *Tell me more! How do you make a poll and a word cloud out of this? Let me show you. I have another idea. We could do it this way perhaps. Let's try!*

In September 2021, we held a two-day event with people from all over the world. Again, we learned, we laughed, and we celebrated.

Now I am the one who helps others through the same journey, and I agree that you cannot help others past the place you have not gone yourself—something that I learned in coach training.

I am now quoting Catarina Kentell, who supported me in saying, "You can do everything online that you could do face to face, except one thing—and that is something you should not do anyway in business contexts. That's hugging and kissing if you're wondering."

So, where am I at now?

I hope the online work stays and grows. If it does, I will be able to grow more internationally, which is part of my vision.

I can continue to grow a more extensive network and continue learning.

Because of how my professional landscape has changed, I am free to work from anywhere globally and combine work and free time, and I love that freedom.

I do want to meet people face to face when it is meaningful, and it often is.

I am curious about what the next year will bring as I continue designing learning journeys for others.

You may be wondering: What happened to the things I thought were not possible when designing workshops? Once I changed my way of thinking, I was able to see my "technologically confined" world from a whole new angle and realize the possibilities. For example:

- Fishbowl exercises can be done by having cameras turned on and off and using different galley views.
- Team exercises can be done with Google Docs, writing fairy tales together.
- Whiteboards can be used with tools such as Miro.com and Mural.com.
- Voting sheets and surveys are easy to create with Menti.com or Howspace.
- Escape rooms work online; there are several. Just Google the term.
- Using a flipped classroom model is much easier using Howspace as the platform.
- Mingling and managing groups moving in and out of the room is easily done in Spatial Chat.
- Cool meeting rooms where all can share can be designed in Wonder.me.
- WhatsApp groups can support learning and be in group rooms if all else fails.
- Walks and Talks can be done over the phone.

Creative check-ins and outs are found in tscheck.in.

These are just a few examples, and there are many more. Feel free to contact me with your best suggestions and learning experiences.

You may have learned other things beyond how to change your attitude and your work methods. Here are a few reflective questions you can ask yourself and your teammates to help you realize how you've evolved during such a challenging period:

- What have you learned about yourself during the last 1.5 years?
- What has become more or less important for you during COVID?
- What are some new perspectives that you see now?
- What small steps can you celebrate now as you look back?
- Who are your best supporters and teachers (and why)?
- What "Monkey Mind" thought will you stop listening to now?

Good luck with this and your ongoing journeys through the "Change Curve."

12

2

Bringing a Traditional Two-Day Workshop to Life Virtually

By Karin Ovari

Safety Leader & Team Creator | Future Human Connection
Designer | Psychological Safety Aficionado
Newburgh, Scotland

"Safety is not a priority. Make safety part of your DNA."

This case study tells the story of how to bring a traditional two-day workshop to life during a global pandemic with outstanding success. Not only is this case study about exploring new tools for global delivery but it is also about how to create a truly global conversation around organisational safety.

The Beginning… November 2019, Scotland

[the client]: Hi, Karin, would you like to help us design our two-day Safety Leadership Workshop? Over the next two years, we will be rolling it out across the globe in key locations in Europe and Africa, the Americas, and the Asia Pacific. The first workshops will kick off in Aberdeen, Scotland.

[me]: Well, of course, the answer was *Hell, yes* (as my C-IQ colleague Tanja would say) because:

1. Being invited to bring my experience, plus elements of Conversational Intelligence©, including neuroscience, into the mix is exciting.

2. This represented another opportunity to make a difference to a global organisation looking to expand and become an industry leader—safety culture is an integral part of that vision.

The overall programme looks at the organisation's safety culture, including safety leadership and managing teams for success (on time and safely). It is a unique programme as there is only one PowerPoint slide, seven posters, and a very cool workbook.

February 2020, Aberdeen
(Cohorts 1 and 2)

The workshop includes a gorgeous venue, stunning views, and fabulous food, including homemade ice cream made from locally grown strawberries. And a tour of the strawberry farm, which was interesting.

The participants are primarily local and UK-based. As you can imagine, there are lots of flip charts and round tables designed for groups of four to five people for maximum communication and group work. Activities include storytelling and sharing, a set of floor mats representing the Safety Culture Maturity Ladder, little wooden people for team mapping, and many more flip-chart moments. And, of course, individual reflective moments for taking notes within their very well-designed workbooks. (We all know what happens to the majority of these.)

The programme is immersive, based on experiential learning, and designed for co-creative learning. The participants are guided and contribute to the whole—a modern approach to learning.

At the end of the second day, there are many flip charts with great information. We [facilitators] promise to capture the key points and return to the participants in some way for their ongoing learning and memories of all their hard work. Anyone who has taken home (or to the office) those end-of-day flip charts knows what this means—work and lots of it, which is often not included in the pricing and design of the programme.

To be clear, in the world I work in, very few people happily volunteer to attend these types of workshops. They are generally "voluntold" (told to come voluntarily). There is often a good deal of resistance to start with, and we facilitators must be engaging and grab the audience's attention pretty darn quickly, or else doing so becomes like pulling teeth. I am happy to announce that I and my co-facilitator are very good at what we do.

The workshop was a great success, with many participants enjoying the design, topics, and interactions—well done, Team.

End of March 2020, Americas (Cohorts 3 and 4)

We successfully conducted two more workshops.

Sadly, I did not go on this trip; however, my co-facilitator and client did and barely made it back to the UK as the world went into major COVID-19 lockdown in early April.

And that was the end of that.

April to August 2020

Just as the world went into major COVID-19 lockdown, the world of virtual events sprang to life. Webinars were on every corner (metaphorically speaking) and insanely dull for the most part. In addition, many coaching and training clients were closing their doors on anything face-to-face or in physical locations; so, clients, facilitators, and coaches alike were scrambling to recreate the face-to-face events virtually, with varying degrees of success.

The world and organisations pushed all their daily norms of operation to the side as they either put employees on furlough (leave) or sent them home with their computers (shock, horror) to continue working. And, as evidence suggests, with tremendous success. Interestingly, the concept of "remote" or "flexible" ways of working is a twenty-year-old one.

There were many reasons why, up to this time, the idea for

most organisations was just a bit hard and is not one for this chapter to explore.

My favourite meme of the time asked this question, "Who led your company's digital transformation?"

1. CEO
2. CTO
3. COVID-19

I sense we all know the answer to that question. Overnight, the IT department had to trust employees with computers and treat them as responsible adults. The CEOs had to relinquish control and *trust* that everyone would still perform—the term "responsible adult" comes to mind again.

Let's move on and learn why I shared the above scenario.

On the 29th of February, a colleague tagged me on LinkedIn to join a group of global facilitators and create a virtual event. We would share concepts, ideas, facilitation skills, collaboration tools (this occurred during the early days of the plethora of collaboration tools that now exist), and much more. The idea was simple enough—let's create an experiential virtual event. It was a resounding success. A lot had to do with timing and the fantastic twenty-eight people who pulled it together in just three weeks.

At the heart of this story is a digital facilitation platform called Howspace, which transformed how we now deliver the two-day global Safety Leadership Workshop. There is a saying that it takes ten thousand hours to master something well. Malcolm Gladwell, author of the popular book *Outliers,* wrote that it takes ten thousand hours to become an expert in anything. I did that in three weeks (or rather, it felt that way), and I have learned a lot more since then. They call me a Howspace superuser. I fell in love with the platform, and it has become core to my business and how I operate now.

A brave new world emerges.

April 2020: Conversation with My Client

As you can imagine, way back in April 2020, my client stopped the programme dead in its tracks. However, during creating the virtual event (called Virtual Collaborations), I realised that there might well be a way to continue delivering the Safety Leadership programme around the globe.

So, I spent a weekend creating a digital version of the programme, focusing on recreating the experiential activities. When ready, I called my client and suggested I may have a way to continue the good work we started and, therefore, keep moving forward. Safety Culture and Leadership programmes are essential for safety-critical organisations (think oil rigs, fast rail, airlines, nuclear plants, etc.). And it is crucial to my client personally.

We met via Zoom. I demonstrated what was possible, and my client loved it.

But during the meeting, the client says, "This [pandemic] will all come to an end soon, so let's see what happens as it might be hard to get the concept accepted by the other senior leaders."

I waited and continued my journey with creating and learning more about digital facilitation and all its possibilities. Today, I am a Howspace Certified Digital Transformation Agent.

August 2020: Okay, This COVID Thing is Not Going Anywhere

My client calls me and says the magic words, "Let's do this." I then considered two questions: What needs to happen? How can we design the programme for continued global rollout?

Happy days. I went about designing and teaching this new way of delivery. We recreated the Safety Culture Maturity Ladder using polls and images (people used to stand somewhere on the ladder [floor mats] physically). So, by using polls and chat widgets, we recreated the experience and improved how to harvest (capture) the conversations by asking the individual to select the rung of the ladder and why they positioned themselves there. Next, the conversation moves into a whole group dialogue. And the more introverted are now contributing to the discussion in the written word for all to see.

And we use AI (artificial intelligence) and machine learning to summarise the discussions.

Remember all those flip charts we used to try to capture everyone's thoughts? Well, the participants themselves contribute to the harvest using their language and input summarised in real-time.

Digital facilitation is a facilitator's dream and incredibly more efficient. So, an exercise that used to take two hours is now done in forty minutes, with better output and discussion.

One of the enormous benefits of Zoom (and yes, there are other tools) is that we get to see everyone at the same time, and because we are all in the same shape, it becomes more inclusive and a safe space for connection. Granted, it does take a different set of facilitation skills.

The programme is still a two-day workshop at this stage. Yes, we have people online for up to seven hours per day, including good breaks, of course. However, the programme has evolved as we have included pre-work and post-work and coaching into the mix. All of which are easier to manage in the virtual realm. More on that later.

September 2020: Cohort 5: First Digitally Facilitated Programme

Wow, wow, wow, what a huge success. Our Cohort 5 participant feedback says it all. (Unedited besides spelling and confidentiality)

- *It is better than being in a room.*
- *I am hearing other people's thoughts and ideas.*
- *Enthusiastic, engaging, and well-constructed course. Interesting to listen to the views of others at different levels of the organisation. Breakout rooms are very useful.*
- *I liked the online format—surprisingly, particularly the ability to mix internationally.*
- *The honest and open conversations with my colleagues from around the globe.*

- *Energise software (Howspace) is impressive and encourages further training.*

I was so nervous, as you can imagine. A lot was riding on the success of this first digital programme as the possible way forward to deliver around the globe. The only vital considerations are time zone and connectivity from various locations at any one time.

What did we learn in this first digital cohort?

Bringing people together from different but close time zones meant we could include people from other regions and departments to improve sharing similar concerns. Fostering the sense of "we are not alone" creates a global community of safety ambassadors rather than just regional.

Other challenges, such as childcare, disabilities, caring for others, etc., are all considered, allowing for greater programme participation.

By bringing people together from different regions and offices, we are provided the ability to broaden the knowledge pool. In addition, insights are derived from various organisational cultural norms, contributing to the organisational culture.

Overall, we found the programme to be more inclusive and considerate of all personality types, from extroverted to introverted.

All of the above is often very difficult to achieve when running workshops in physical locations—the time and cost of travel and accommodation for all the participants is prohibitive for most organisations.

Virtual learning is good for business and morally justifiable, benefiting people, profit, and the planet through reduced travel (carbon emissions), decreased costs, and time-saving. These elements alone are good arguments for more virtual learning rather than less as organisations and their way of working move toward flexible and remote working.

September 2021: Where are We Now, and What has Changed?

We will soon roll out Cohort 12 as the programme continues its success. Has it evolved? Yes, it has.

What started as a two-day workshop with a ninety-minute prelude (programme introduction) two days before the two-day workshop has evolved into a four-month immersive programme. Based on the "before, during, and after" concept of shared learning.

Today, participants are invited to complete a self-paced pre-learning module called the Prelude and guided through a set of activities to:

1. help them become familiar with the digital platform
2. highlight any potential technical challenges
3. capture their thoughts on elements such as "safety vision" and what they want to get from the programme and what they will bring to the programme—all this data we use during the day-one live workshop. The day-one live workshop focuses on their individual beliefs and perceptions of safety leadership.

The original two-day live workshop days have been split,

allowing for deeper reflection between days and a 1:1 coaching session per participant. Then, they come back for the day-two live workshop, where the focus is on Team. So, how do they, as leaders, keep the Team safe?

We then split the whole group into two smaller groups, and the journey continues with a series of small, group-facilitated coaching sessions over the following six weeks. All this ends with a final wrap-up 1:1 coaching session.

The client is thrilled with the overall progression of the programme, as are the participants.

Participant feedback from more recent cohorts (unedited besides spelling and confidentiality):

- *The program is well put together and brought together, not just the UK people.*
- *Robust conversations*
- *Breakout rooms were good to meet others and exchange views.*
- *Interactive, a chance to meet people from all over the world*
- *Multiple regions in one "room"*
- *The fact we are unknowingly creating our training content*
- *Similar issues across different regions; we can relate and target this together.*
- *The ability to say what's on your mind. The coaching was really great, and it gave me more insight into myself—my leadership abilities, etc.*
- *I enjoyed that the programme allows collaboration with others from around the globe instead of those from your specific region only.*

- *The programme was totally unexpected. I didn't expect to enjoy the process or the interaction, being a bit of an introvert.*

Technology

The technology we use needs to be simple, effective, and ubiquitous across devices.

The tools we choose to use are:

- **Zoom** for the synchronous real-time connection, and
- **Howspace**, a robust, browser-based application for digital facilitation and asynchronous connection where dialogue matters.

I will assume that you are well familiar with Zoom or similar tools at this time and have no need for a deeper explanation. There are, of course, good facilitation tools, tips, and tricks that we employ to make the participant experience easy and enjoyable. Breakout rooms are critical for intimate dialogue and group work.

Often, the challenge is how to capture the learnings from those breakout rooms and groups. But again, there are a plethora of excellent collaboration tools on the market, and even a simple shared document can be very effective. We chose Howspace Superchat Widget and AI to capture those conversations and learnings.

Good digital facilitation requires intuitive, simple, noiseless (not too many bells and whistles) tools and applications. Howspace fits that bill beautifully.

It is easy to design (fully customisable); no training is required for the participants to become active and engaged. Moreover, it has terrific AI (artificial intelligence), allowing for real-time word clouds, conversation summaries, and much more.

Remember all those flip charts from the physical events? Now it is done by the participants and machine learning in real-time.

Using a tool such as Howspace allows for the entire learning journey, open dialogue, and community building, driving engagement *before* the event (live workshop) and *during* the live workshop for sharing, reflection, and social learning. And it supports the *after*-workshop engagement by developing the learning community for all participants past and present.

https://www.howspace.com/learning-platform

Key findings

- Improved diversity, equity, and inclusion
- Hearing from all participants either by voice or written
- Using a digital facilitation tool that is a game-changer
- Offering a safe space for all
- Improved data capture and sharing
- Easier group sharing session
- Enhanced sharing of organisational knowledge for the greater good

- Community building
- Cost-effective for people, planet, and business

Summary

The solution to continuing the rollout of a global, organisation-wide safety leadership programme is driven by the need for a changing world and has become the standard delivery method moving forward, regardless of any relaxing pandemic constraints.

The cost savings have been enormous due to reduced travel and accommodation needs. As a result, there is a more significant opportunity for cross-cultural inclusion, diversity, and knowledge sharing, allowing for a genuinely international safety culture change programme.

3

Learning From Loss: How a Traumatic Public Event Inspired a Safe Virtual Workspace

By Deborah Goldstein

Coach | Facilitator | Consultant
Cold Spring, New York, USA

"Trust Takes Years to Build, Seconds to Break and Forever to Repair."
~Dhar Mann

At a time when every person on the planet was connected by COVID-19, a single incident divided us. George Floyd's murder changed the world, and it changed my understanding of the realities of building trust.

June 1, 2020

Listening Circles: "Absorbing the Impact of Anti-Black Racism… and Moving Forward Together"

The racial tension spreading across North America impacts each of us, regardless of race, ethnicity, religion, or culture. This is a pivotal time in our history, and together, we will benefit by supporting each other as we process and make sense of these current events.

Please join us in the safe space of The Campfire, where you can commune with your colleagues and share questions, thoughts, emotions, and ideas. Processing together can be both comforting and powerful. As a community, we can move from helplessness to hopefulness and become stronger by leveraging the opportunities presented during this moment in our history.

I drafted this invitation, inviting the 6,500 employees of a North American municipality to a Zoom session days after George Floyd's murder. I wrote it, but I wasn't sure if I was being truthful about the "promised outcome." Hopeful? Yes. But most certainly not confident in our ability to create the safe space needed for a genuine connection. After all, this facilitation was like nothing I'd ever done before. We were hoping to create a safe container during a week of protests and continued emotional volatility. Everyone was on edge, our amygdalas, the part of the brain responsible for initiating "fight or flight," were "wagging." My co-facilitator and I needed to create safety quickly—and by web conference no less!

I had been working with this municipality since March. Our team was contracted to help the city workers acclimate, adapt, and succeed while working from home. I knew a small portion of the workforce and had gotten a sense of the leadership's temperament. I was actually preparing over the

Memorial Day weekend for our last Learning Day, with the client's workforce to be held on June 5th, when our contact reached out, requesting an urgent change of plans.

This was the request (all names, save my own, have been changed):

Dear Tom and Deborah,

I'm writing with an "urgent" request for Friday for an additional session or dedicated space/time on the Campfire site to discuss the anti-Black racism that is at the center of our experience right now. It's been personally weighing down on me and I have set up a space for the HR folks on Thursday during our regular weekly huddle. I wasn't sure if I wanted to do something on the large platform of Learning Days. However, in exploring the safest way to gently take a step in that direction, I received some validations for creating a space similar to past timed discussions on the Campfire site.

It would be most critical that the facilitator for this session is a Black (ideally living in North America) expert in facilitating a sensemaking session because in my opinion (I'm not an expert on this), the first validation for the audience for such a session would be the facilitator. And the greatest skill set needed for this first session would be less about being an expert in diversity or anti-Black racism and more about allowing people the grace, space, and time to share out loud how they are processing what's happening in the US and Canada. I don't know everyone on your roster of facilitators, but I believe Sally Smith would do a masterful job of facilitating this discussion. I would love it if Deborah could co-facilitate that with

Sally; that would be ideal in my opinion! I'm happy to welcome other recommendations you may have.

Could we please embed this in the agenda on the website and title it around "Making sense of the anti-Black racism and find ways to process it/move forward"…something along those lines? I want the largest majority of registrants to be able to see why all of us, whatever racial identity we may have, could benefit from this safe space to process this information because it impacts us all.

Last but not least, the chosen facilitator would be invited to thoroughly review our Diversity and Inclusion strategy that was based on an organizational assessment that noted the perceived discrimination experienced by our Black employees.

Please let me know how I can help. It is very, very critical to do this well.

Most sincerely,
Leena Mehta

Setting the Scene

The end of May 2020 was such a raw time. I was running on fumes, working too much, exhausted, and scared. And that was before the disturbing incident that took place in Minneapolis on May 25, 2020.

Upon receiving this email on Sunday, May 31, I became acutely aware of the importance of this session. Leena had stated the obvious and had even accentuated her point by using two "verys." We had to pull it together quickly in order to deliver an impactful and meaningful discussion. Although this discussion would be a totally different animal from what I was used to, the preparation and mindset would be familiar to me.

The Strategy Meeting

I'd pored over the Diversity and Inclusion strategy as per Leena's offer. I also had a sense of their cultural language after working with this municipality in a daily capacity over the prior three months.

During a meeting on Tuesday, June 2, my cofacilitator and I shared our thoughts about the purpose of and our roles during this Listening Circle. We voiced the importance of a fluid structure and giving the participants space. We articulated the desire to act as guardrails, to gently guide this workforce through a process of creating a sense of safety in the "room" so each had the headspace to share what was in their heart as well as listen and learn and support each other. We also wanted to give them the opportunity to state what they wanted to see within their municipality in response to Floyd's murder and what they would commit to making happen. Deep down, I was concerned about everything we didn't know. Would our guardrails be mowed down?

I have developed a practice of considering three questions before any engagement or discussion:

1.   How do I want to present?
2.   What information do I want to convey?
3.   How do I want others to feel?

I wanted to present, or show up, as a guardian of safe space—this was the key to the crucial session. I had to alter my mindset about the second question as I need not provide anything *but* the space in this instance. This is a foreign concept to me. I wanted to reframe or change my mindset from "creating and providing value" to holding space.

After some discussion, our answer to the third question was that we wanted people to feel:

- welcomed.
- valued.
- respected.
- heard.

Okay, now that we had defined our aspirational vision, the next step was to assess the situation.

A mantra from my restaurant years: "When you control the knowns, the unknowns become more manageable." So, what did I know?

The Knowns

In the best of situations, when working within an organization, trust is hard to build and even more challenging to maintain.

A virtual workplace has another set of challenges:

- If people are on screen, you can't read body language.
- Bad digital connections provide your brain a lot of opportunities to jump to conclusions.
- Looking into someone's eyes on the screen leads to a sense of disconnection because you can't look at the person and see them looking back at you due to the camera's position. And creating the online perception that you're looking into the other's eyes by looking at the little green light just feels inauthentic!

- You don't know anything about the people you're connecting with beyond what you see in the small space that the webcam reveals, which often includes a synthetic backdrop.

The mission of my company, DRIVEN Professionals, is to help organizations thrive in the twenty-first century. My interpretation of this is to create a psychologically safe workplace so people can be fully engaged, creative, and productive. Creating safe space has historically been a one-dimensional struggle; people are fearful in their workplace of being fired or reprimanded, embarrassed, or passed over. In the Listening Circle, there was another dimension of danger. People were not only fearful for their psychological safety but also for their personal safety. We were in physical danger due to COVID-19, and we were all raw while reading about, hearing, and seeing peaceful protests, riots, and police violence during that time.

The Unknowns

We were also in the dark about who to expect during that session. How many people would show up? What would be their state of mind? What emotions were people feeling? What would they be expecting? How could we "read them" and connect with them if they attended the session with their cameras off? These concerns were based on our previous experience facilitating virtual experiences with this workforce.

In this crucial situation, I felt the extra stress of a question, "Are we *sure* we can create a safe container for this conversation?" I've always worn my responsibility heavily on my shoulders. And Leena's request was both humbling and terrifying. My inner critic was roaring!

Logistical Caution

Another challenge of a Zoom room is how people could silently "drop in at any time." We considered what could happen if people came in lacking context in the middle of a potentially heavy or volatile discussion. When I raised the issue, I was referencing the not-so-distant past, when I'd frequently attended networking events. I found that when I arrived early, I was able to ease into discussions and conversations. When I arrived late, the vibe had been set, and a palpable energy had been built. I found it trickier to get involved in the conversation at that point. I wouldn't want someone who is in distress because of the pandemic and Floyd's murder to get triggered by "dropping in" to a heated moment in time. So, we decided that we'd have the discussion in a breakout room. This meant that people would arrive at the session and be "sent" to one room, where the facilitated discussion would take place. A little clumsy, but it was still attractive for two reasons:

1. We could lock the session if needed.
2. We had someone at the gate inviting late arrivals to give some context before they entered the discussion area.

Priming Myself: From the "We" to the "Me"

Before entering any coaching or facilitation interaction, I take time to check in with myself. This means tuning into my emotions, state of mind, physical state, and what could potentially get in the way of being "in-flow" with the client(s). I want to hold a neutral space, with no agenda and no clogged filter due to my "stuff."

There were a lot of checkpoints to consider:

- In the words of Vincent Van Gogh, "Let's not forget that the little emotions are the captains of our lives, and we obey them without realizing it." I may not realize what I'm doing in the moment, but there is one thing that has become blatantly apparent to me. When I'm in a toxic state, I know it affects how I see the world. And because my thoughts affect my behaviors and actions, my toxicity will affect how others act.

- Blind Spots: I know through Judith E. Glaser's work that we don't see clearly under stress. Judith was my mentor and the creator of Conversational Intelligence®, a protocol that has informed the foundation of my coaching practice. I had to acknowledge that this was a stressful situation in many dimensions. I was aware that due to my exhaustion, my thinking was distorted, and my emotions could easily take the lead. And unless I'm aware and present, I am neurochemically unable to be fully empathic.

- These circumstances were unusual. My co-facilitator and I were struggling ourselves. Usually we, as facilitators, get to remain objective. In this case, it was personal to us, too.

- I'd just finished co-facilitating a "feel good" deeply introspective session. Looking back to the transition to our Listening Circle, it was like walking into an emergency room from a stroll on the beach.

- I was painfully aware of my greatest blind spot: Each of us humans believe, "Everyone sees the world as I see the world." It was important not to make assumptions about how *anyone* saw, thought, and felt about the situation at hand.

- I was also sensitive about the perception and reception of myself as a White person asked to facilitate. I took on the support role for my co-facilitator. Similar to the power of having outside facilitators as opposed to leadership facilitating this intimate session, my foreign status was a benefit to the situation. My race, however, was a disadvantage.

I had been journaling about all these dimensions over the week. Although I was unsure of how others were going to show up, at least I had an intellectual handle on how *I* could show up. And with that knowledge, at 4:30 p.m., when my workshop ended, I knew I had about seven minutes to embody the presence I wanted to project for the 4:45 p.m. start of the one-hour Listening Circle.

Thank goodness for my rituals!

Priming the Space

- Physical Space: I prepared two liters of sparkling water for this one-hour session and arranged them, along with my pen and notepaper. I checked my lighting and the angle of my camera. There's nothing worse when someone is vulnerably sharing than to see the top of someone else's head.

- I stretched and breathed for about five minutes—long, slow, luxurious breaths, totally present and connected to each repetition of breathing.
- I asked myself once again the three questions that help ground me intentionally in the present:
  - How do we want to show up?
  - What information do we want to convey?
  - How do we want people to feel at the end of the meeting?

The Campfire Session

At 4:45 p.m. sharp, we opened the doors to the Zoom room. We spent five minutes in a gentle welcome pattern. This took two forms of communication. Sally, speaking warmly, steadily, and slowly, welcomed the group. I was copying and pasting the welcome message a few times as people joined, knowing that when they did, they couldn't see messages prior to entry.

We also verbalized a warm welcome to different groups as we continued to speak and write targeted messages to gain some context and create early connections. "Did you attend the discussion exclusive to Black employees of the munic-ipality this afternoon?" was one of them, along with many welcome statements to people we knew by name, thanks to the work we'd been doing since March.

Creating Safe Space

We were scheduled for a sixty-minute discussion. At 4:50 p.m., we started by asking three deliberately paced questions to the growing group for over five minutes. We invited responses in the chat box.

As the responses to the first question from the predominantly anonymous audience (not too many people with cameras on) began to trickle in, I read quickly, and at the same time, I intentionally slowed down my breathing. Patience, certainly not a virtue of mine, is likewise non-negotiable when it comes to creating the space we need. It's counterintuitive but true.

How are you entering the space?

The first ninety seconds brought information about the emotional state of some in our midst:

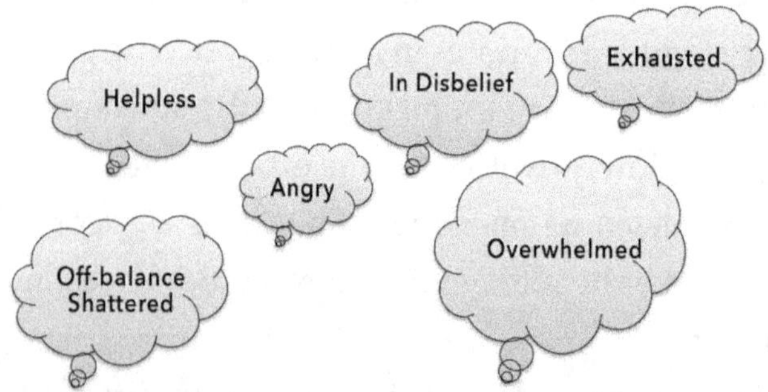

What do you need for this to be a safe space?

As facilitators, we must maintain curiosity, the ability to listen without letting our biases interfere, and truly understand (stand under) others' realities. We can't afford to let the number-one blind spot to good communication get in our way: that "everyone sees the world as I see the world." I learned about the Platinum Rule forty years after hearing the Golden Rule and was always amused that the Golden Rule is all about you, whereas the Platinum Rule is truly about serving others.

This question allows people to be vulnerable.

Why did you come?

Then, there was a curiosity about what we could deliver. Why did they come? What were they hoping for?

Sallie began to pick up on the chat box comments slowly, rather than filling space with words. She allowed those in the room to fill *their* space. Then we asked for voices. "Would anyone like to share what's on their mind?" Silence.

This is the most frustrating part of virtual work. Seven seconds seem like an eternity. "Breathe, patience, let the silence expand. It's okay." I found myself coaching myself during the eerie silences.

When I began to wonder if I was lost in space (did my Wi-Fi freeze?), a Black male participant unmuted himself to share his thoughts. He expressed his anger and exhaustion about the hopelessness he felt toward those blind to the realities of White privilege.

This led to the natural question, "What is White privilege?" This classic example of "double-clicking" gracefully opens people's lenses to better understand others' realities. This type of question allows us to explore a concept more widely and deeply. If you recall, the number-one blind spot we humans have is believing everyone sees the world the same way *we* do.

The answers were fascinating. What was even more impressive was that no facilitated definition was ever offered. Instead, Sally asked, "Would anyone like to share a situation or instance where you've not been seen, heard, or treated with respect?"

Clearly, psychological safety had been created. The stories that followed were from the heart and received with empathy and warmth. The compassion of the group was palpable through the chat box; participants began writing to offer their support to the courageous folks who shared their unfathomable, yet considering what was happening across the country, all-too-real injustices.

These first confessions organically moved to more people sharing stories and the outpouring of support. It was a powerful group catharsis, and yet, still sobering, with the comment that these sessions should be mandatory. I listened, blown away by the vulnerability of the storytellers and moved by the support in the chat box. Many of these people were strangers to each other, coming together as a reassuring raft in a storm.

Sally masterfully segued to questions about proposed solutions and actions these participants were willing to commit to.

We began to wrap up after ninety minutes, although I'm convinced that if we hadn't, people would have stayed on the line for hours. There was a feeling of catharsis. As people left comments in the chat box, the shift in the energy of the virtual room gained dimension. I felt a sense of hopefulness, community, understanding, support, and togetherness. Some closing remarks from participants included:

- *"Please let us not let this momentum end! We have the attention, we have the numbers, we need the action. Thank you everyone for sharing your stories and perspectives."*
- *"This was a great session and thank you to those who shared their personal stories."*
- *"Thank you immensely for providing space today and to those who shared and contributed to the conversation."*
- *"Thank you. It was very eye-opening to hear some of the stories. It's one thing to hear something on the news, but it's a totally different story to hear how people you know and work with have been made to feel."*
- *"I am more hopeful after listening today."*

In Hindsight

During my traditional debrief practice, I recognized how fortuitous we were to have conducted this session virtually. Although, leading up to the Listening Circle, I had been concerned that we would not be able to create a safe space via Zoom, in hindsight, I recognize that the virtual venue was indeed the ideal stage for our sensitive topic of discussion. And I'll be forever grateful that Sally and I intentionally took the pre-Listening Circle steps to maximize the home-field advantage for everyone involved.

Here are my hindsight notes:

1. We were able to "meet people where they are" literally! Anyone employed by this municipality was invited to attend the discussion from the privacy and safety of their own home. They could share without exposing

themselves. They could show up without having to curb their emotions. I don't know if I'd have ventured into a meeting like this in person, one that could be emotional, vulnerable, even volatile.

2. I was better able to adhere to ethical coaching. Coaches are trained to be detached from client issues. We work to stay out of the problem while maintaining perspective. In this instance, every person on the planet was emotionally involved with this situation. Sally and I benefited by way of detachment thanks to the virtual environment.

3. We also benefited from a neurochemical perspective. Esteemed psychiatrist Dr. Stephen Porges, author of *The Polyvagal Theory*, says, "When others are near us and get emotional, it's contagious." In other words, we take on the vibes more intensively. We feel it in a virtual room, but it isn't as intense, and we're better able to ground ourselves when we're not physically sharing space with others. We can more easily down-regulate our agitated emotions.

4. Those who courageously shared were flooded with support, thanks to the chat box. Not only were the written words a source for empathy and compassion, but they also inspired others to share.

5. Sally was able to verbally highlight and mirror the positive comments that were coming in. She could be selective in her reflections and had the potential to refocus the conversation more powerfully than if we were in-person.

6. The one thing that didn't work in our favor was a result of being strategic and deliberate in setting up a breakout room to protect late arrivers. I learned too late that even as a co-host, I wasn't able to mute people in the breakout room.
7. CAN'T MUTE in B/O rooms!

Looking to the Future

The COVID-19 pandemic has devastated the world in multiple dimensions. It has changed our lives forever. Once an egg yolk has been broken, it can't be put back together. Hence, the gratitude toward scrambled eggs. We will not go "back to normal," but rather, embrace the next normal again and again. One of the positive outcomes of this pandemic has been the success of virtual work for some. At the outset, there was much doubt about how people could feel connected and build trust via video chat. Thanks to my experience with the June 5, 2020 Listening Circle, there is no doubt in my mind trust and intimacy can be built virtually. Looking ahead, when teams are thoughtful and strategic, meetings, trainings, and everyday interactions can be fruitful and effective virtually. In fact, certain situations benefit from virtual interaction.

4

How to Create Dynamic Virtual Presentations and Seminars

By Linda Keller

Leadership and Team Development | Transition Coaching
Cross-Cultural Business Communication | Life Coaching
Herrenberg, Germany

Can a presentation be like a good conversation when it is virtual? During the pandemic, I was challenged with substituting a face-to-face presentation seminar with an online training session. If you are a coach and want to support your clients to give dynamic presentations online, are interested in improving or simply reviewing your own general presentation skills, or are a trainer thinking of giving presentation seminars online, here are a few insights based on my experience.

The Contract: how it came about

It all began one morning after I had just finished an online coaching session with an executive. The phone rang. It was a

German company asking me to give a three-day presentation seminar online in English. The seminar had originally been planned as a face-to-face event, but due to the pandemic, now had to be online, and they wanted me to do it in MS Teams. The trainer originally contracted to give the seminar had pulled out, and I had been recommended. I have worked with clients in various countries, and working globally has always meant being able to work remotely—even before the days of Zoom, et al. It was nothing new to me; however, the difference was that when the pandemic struck, everyone was in lockdown, and there was suddenly no more working or presenting face-to-face. From one day to the next, almost everything was remote, and the technology to facilitate this was quickly improving.

I was interested in running the training for them because I am passionate about supporting people in their ability to communicate. It was, however, rather short notice, and I was not used to using MS Teams—my largest concern at the time. I knew Zoom well and was comfortable working with it. I asked for time to reflect and said I'd get back to them.

I was excited and basically knew I had to give it a go. I asked around to see if any of my colleagues had experience using Microsoft Teams, but none did. Oh, well. I would work out how to use Teams somehow. After all, this would not be the first time I had jumped in at the deep end and swum. I also sensed this would not be the first time a company would insist that I use MS Teams, especially as Teams had recently also integrated the possibility for breakout rooms.

By now, many of you know what breakout rooms are, but for any who may not, they are a way of creating different rooms and assigning people from the main room (session) to one of the other rooms, enabling small groups to work together. As host, you can then enter each room and facilitate in the same way as you would if you were physically present. As far as I know, Zoom was the first platform to have breakout rooms. Now they seem to be ubiquitous, and almost all the main platforms have them—it is just slightly easier to manage them in some platforms than in others.

As I pondered all this, I remembered how often I had asked myself: Why, when even before the COVID-19 pandemic around 80 percent of international business presentations were virtual, did most presentation training seem to focus on classical, face-to-face presentation skills? That might partly be attributed to the success of TED Talks; after all, they made an enormous impact on what people today consider to be a good presentation. And let's face it, who would not like to be able to get up and give a compelling presentation in front of a live audience? To feel the thrill, the power of grabbing and maintaining attention, be entertaining, and give the audience a memorable experience?

The COVID-19 pandemic had—and has—in no way changed the fascination for TED Talks, but it was largely why the demand for online presentation training suddenly shot up. Many people are still working in home offices and have almost forgotten the last time they gave, or were invited, to a live presentation. In addition, most businesses are practically relying on the fact that our virtual work life is—at least partly—here to stay. I, too, believe that when our working lives start to normalise again, we will not be going back to what we had before, at least not immediately. Employers and employees now both understand the benefits of a home office. More importantly, they are now also beginning to realise that different skill sets are required to get the best out of the new situation and their employees.

Even though at the beginning, managers were worried about their team's productivity, they have, in many cases, actually seen productivity rise, thus eliminating that concern. In addition, they have also realized tremendous opportunities to save costs on rent, travel expenses, canteens, etc.

Their current challenges are in discovering how they can support their employees and help them make a stronger impact online. They are more aware of how important it is to be able to build and maintain relationships online.

They now want answers to questions such as, "How can our employees be compelling online? How can they drive decisions online in this VUCA (volatility, uncertainty, complexity, and ambiguity) world, where they may never have met the decision-makers face-to-face—and may not meet them in the next few months or even years? How can they build strong teams when they are now also working locally with new colleagues they have never met personally? How can they remain creative?"

The more I thought about it all, the more I became convinced I had to give it a shot! After all, what did I have to lose? I could really only benefit. Even if I didn't make a total success of it, I would definitely learn a lot I could use in the future and also enhance my own presentation skills. I had recently given over two hundred hours of online university lectures—including some training on giving international presentations, and the feedback on that was positive. I had also given several three-day online intercultural business communication and team-building workshops as well as many successful individual transition coaching sessions. I felt I had a solid technical skill set and a fair idea of how to make the transfer. Reflecting on all this gave me the confidence I needed, and I agreed to run the three-day online presentation training course.

Planning

First, I thought about how to plan the course. What would be the same? What would I need to change? I knew several things would be different but also that the basic structure would remain quite similar, so I decided to take the structure of an in-person presentation training course and contemplate the various individual differences as I went along. From my experience working and presenting online, and the courses I had taken myself, I had learned the following:

- Everything takes longer in the virtual world.
- Everything is more difficult and tiring when body language cues from the audience are missing.
- Concentration spans are shorter—people cannot listen for longer than five to seven minutes at a time.

- You are permanently competing with a barrage of other things that pop up on the participants' screens, all vying for their attention.
  All this meant I had to:
- Plan for less input
- Have more visuals and move through them more quickly
- Be lively; use my voice and as much body language as possible (hands, facial expressions, etc.)
- Be understanding—sympathise with the challenges my participants may be facing and see them through their eyes
- Keep things crisp and clear to avoid misunderstandings
- Engage the audience more often in interactive activities and tasks

I began by looking at the *Why? Who? What?* and *How?* of presenting.

Why?

I am always astonished when people planning to give a presentation concentrate on *what* they want to tell the audience but not *why!* They think of everything they know about the subject but rarely enough about what their *main message* is: what they want the audience to remember and what they want to get the audience to do after the presentation.

The Right Communication Medium

If people think more about their *why*, they may actually decide that a live presentation (online or face-to-face)—is not the best way of conveying the information. So, irrespective of whether online or face-to-face, the first thing you need to consider is whether a presentation is the right communication medium.

Thinking of the *why* helps you consider whether a written document, e.g., a report, an email, a memo, or a letter might suffice or is the best option. That is invariably the case when there is no need to empathise with the audience, when it does not matter to you if you move them from where they are to somewhere else or when you do not feel it necessary to touch the emotions of your audience.

However, if you do mind, if it really does matter to you, and you do want to influence your audience, to move them from here to there, and your objective is to inspire the audience to action by winning over their minds and hearts, you are dealing with a more complex situation, and a richer form of communication will be necessary. In that case, you will want to show empathy, to touch emotions and engage the whole brain of everyone in your audience. So, you will need pictures, facts, and stories. You will need to use your body, face, and voice; in short, you will need to give a dynamic and compelling presentation. All those things are extremely important in face-to-face presentations, and they are at least *twice as important* in online presentations.

Who? The Audience

Knowing *why* you are going to give a presentation will inextricably be linked to *who* you are giving it to. You will not only have a clearer idea of what they want from you, but more importantly, you will also know what you want from them. First, however, you need to get them to want to listen to you.

Grabbing the audience's attention at the beginning and maintaining it during a presentation is paramount, whether it is online or face-to-face. So, first, you need to consider who the audience is. You cannot start to think about or plan anything—not the introduction, the language you are going to use, how to create a good opening, nor the duration or even the content—until you have a clear idea of who your audience is. That means when you consider your audience, you need to ask yourself the following:

- Who are they? More senior in rank? More junior?
- What knowledge do they have on the subject?
- What resistance might they have for your topic?
- Where do they come from? (e.g., country, company, industry, etc.)
- Why are they attending? (compulsory, voluntarily)
- What age group?
- What will they be expecting?
- What do you want them to do after the presentation?
- Why are you the right person to give the presentation?

These and other questions are nothing new to anyone who has given or taken part in any form of presentation training. They can be found in the many books that exist on giving presentations; they are what we as trainers and coaches teach and are what we mostly use when we try to prepare for the seminars we give.

When preparing for an online seminar, you come to realise just how vital those questions are. Preparation is key because it is far more challenging to build rapport, empathy, and trust or gain respect and authority when you cannot read the room, when you cannot see or feel people's reactions and are competing with the audience's inboxes, instant messages, text messages, internet browsers, telephones, coffee machines, and maybe even their children or partners. As trainers, we also have to reflect on the participants' own challenges—they may be worried because they do not have a stable or fast enough internet connection. There may be roadworks outside, and the sound of a pneumatic drill or lawnmower might drown out the incoming sound of their loudspeakers. And even without any of these, attention spans are shorter online. This means you as the presenter also have less time to get your message across.

Considering how long your audience can pay attention is vital when preparing for any presentation, especially in an international context. How long people from different cultures are able to listen, even during face-to-face presentations, varies enormously. In his book *When Cultures Collide*, Richard D. Lewis writes about how attention spans differ from culture to culture, from very short to over an hour. According to him, a German or Japanese audience will be quite happy to listen to you for an hour, an American will be bored after thirty minutes, and a Mediterranean or Arabian audience will probably start fidgeting after ten minutes. So, culture cannot be ignored, and knowing *who* the people in your audience are, as well as where they come from, is of utmost importance because it will have a larger impact on the presentation than just its duration.

What? Content

Culture does not only impact the expectations your audience will have in regard to timing but also on *what* kind of information is included and *how* it is delivered. That means that when preparing the content stage, you need to consider aspects such as information, structure, context, formality, emotion, humour, and language. At this stage, questions I ask myself while preparing for any presentation include:

- How much time do I have?
- What information will I include and how much?
- How much context will they want?
- How detailed should the information be?
- How much technical information will I have to include?
- How structured do I need to be?
- How formal/informal?
- Can I use emotion, or do I have to stick purely to facts?
- Does the audience want me to be high-energy and lively or more reserved?
- Can I use humour, or will that be seen as unprofessional, or even worse, potentially misunderstood?
- What language will I be speaking? And what will be the audience's native language? If the language I am speaking is not their native language, how well do they speak that language?

In my case, I had been informed that the members of the seminar were all IT specialists in their thirties, German, and all spoke English well. I knew Germans love and need structure and are very data-oriented. As I mentioned before, they are good listeners, can listen for over an hour, and focus on detailed information, including solid background and technical information. They expect context and quality, and they do not expect to be entertained during a presentation.

I couldn't help reflecting how different it would be if the audience were British! The British do want to be entertained, and as such, humour is always included—presenters will often make jokes about themselves. They want as few figures as possible and nothing too technical. They like a story and expect a message with some sort of emotional appeal. If they have all that, they can happily listen to you for around forty to fifty minutes.

So, what do you think a British person thinks when they have sat through a German presentation? *"Boring,"* *"Information overload," and, "Message got lost in the details!"* are statements I often hear.

And what does a German who sits through a typical British presentation think? *"Too superficial, "Not serious enough,"* and maybe even, *"Flippant."*

So, what if 50 percent of the members of the audience were German and the other 50 percent British? What if you had to give a presentation to ten people, all from different cultural backgrounds, all expecting something else? You would have to find a way of at least meeting their most important expectations.

Luckily, culture is not static, it is dynamic. So, the more we work together globally, the more we build trust and respect each other. The more we can accept there are different ways of doing things, the more we can accept that there is no one right or wrong way, just a lot of different ways, and we can learn to adapt, understand, and appreciate each different way.

How?

While deciding the *what*, we have already, to a certain extent, also been envisaging the *how*. So far, the differences between preparing and delivering face-to-face versus online presentations and trainings have been relatively minor. Then, when we consider how we are going to deliver, we will also find similarities, but the importance of various aspects changes.

Body Language

In face-to-face presentations, we focus on personal presence: how we move, stand, and use our arms, hands, legs, and feet. How we keep eye contact with the audience, and how we use our voice. That is all logical because we know that the audience will be aware of and see it all. So, we practise it when we learn how to give presentations, and during that practice, we are often filmed and given feedback from others. Then, when we give the presentation, we get direct feedback from the audience. We can feel the atmosphere, see whether the audience is listening to us, looking at their mobile phone, or talking to their neighbour, and we can react spontaneously. We can change what we are doing; speak more loudly, quietly, quickly, or slowly; change the subject; do an on-the-spot survey; or even ask people to turn to their neighbour and discuss something.

When presenting online, we focus on our online presence, and all those physical aspects are just as or even more important. Here are some tips to help you.

Make sure you can be seen.

The first thing we are going to look at is how to make an impact. Your face is your biggest tool when it comes to making initial impact, so making sure it can be seen at its best is the first thing you need to focus on. A good way of finding out what you look like is to use your mobile phone. I took my mobile phone, put on my camera as if to take a selfie, and walked around to find out where the most flattering lighting was, where I could be seen most clearly and naturally. I soon realized I had to be facing a window. If light came from the side, which was how I liked working best, I could only see half of my face, and when I had the window behind me, I was in the dark, and my face could not be seen at all.

Create your environment.

Once the lighting is sorted, you focus on how to fill the frame: the picture you are creating of yourself and your environment. At this point, it is important to know that the space between the frame and the top of the head should not be more than a quarter of the total frame's height. I normally go for having around one-fifth of the slide above my head.

There is nothing worse than watching someone whose head only fills the bottom half of the frame.

Next, create your setting. Check what can be seen behind you and keep the backdrop clear and relevant. Remember, you want it to support and enhance your message, and it will be seen behind you for the duration of the presentation.

Using a virtual backdrop can sometimes be advantageous, particularly if you want to use it to give a more corporate feeling. Then you might create a virtual picture of your office or company meeting room with the company logo, for example, and use that as your backdrop. I personally think it is better to have a real backdrop, but if you cannot arrange that, you can also use one of the many virtual backgrounds. Just make sure no one is walking around behind you as they can still be seen through the virtual background—the same goes for you if you get up and move around.

Look into the camera, *not* at the people on your screen.

If you look at the people, the audience sees and so thinks you are looking down. To make people think you are looking at them, you have to look into the camera, which should be positioned at eye level. Talking to the camera is one of the most difficult things to learn as it robs you of the chance to catch a glimpse of any body language cues you might just be able to pick up from the audience. If you find it difficult to talk to the camera, try putting a photo of someone you like talking to directly above the camera and imagine you are talking to them. I did that at the beginning and always chose a photo of someone who was interested in the topic I was talking about. It helped me enormously, and I still do it when I have to talk about something I have not presented before.

Use your face.

Your face is your biggest asset when you want to make an impact. So, keep your listeners interested by *matching* your facial expressions with what you are saying. Also, match your face to your body movements, e.g., when you shrug your shoulders, you may raise your eyebrows, or when you say something is small, you may squint slightly and place your thumb and index finger closer together, or have your arms wide apart and your eyes wide open when talking about something that is very big, etc.

Wear what you would if you were presenting face-to-face.

Choose the kind of clothes you want to wear to achieve the impact you want to make carefully. Wear the same clothes when presenting virtually as you would when delivering to a face-to-face audience. Also, consider that it is not just about what you look like but also about how you feel. Whatever it is you wear, make sure it is suitable but also comfortable.

I took an online presence course myself; in fact, I have taken three. This particular one was run by an actress and theatre director who advised us to wear good shoes as well. I hadn't thought of telling people to expressly do that, but it is true. You are more present and stable when you are wearing shoes. So, even if it is warm outside and you would rather be wearing flip-flops, and nobody is going to see your feet anyway, wear good, comfortable shoes.

Deliver your presentation standing up.

That brings me directly to the next point—energy. Maintaining a high energy level is more important when you are presenting online. You want to keep the audience's attention, but it can be quite challenging to keep it when you do not feel the energy from the audience. When you start to feel tired, you cannot move around the way you can in a face-to-face situation. Despite this, I see most people delivering their presentation sitting down, and after a while, they are often slumped in a chair and look as tired as they must be feeling. By that time, their audience is highly likely to feel just as tired if not more so.

My advice to everyone is to deliver your presentation standing up. You have far more energy and presence and feel much more in command when you are standing. Your voice is stronger, and you can use your hands to make gestures more easily and freely. I ask all the participants in my courses to try it out, and they all really feel the difference. Most of them then immediately decide to stand up when they deliver their next presentation.

Nevertheless, as I mentioned earlier, the camera has to be at eye level. That means you must have your camera and laptop higher too. So, you need a higher table. I started off by placing my laptop on a pile of books; now I have a higher table and a stand for my laptop. And if I have to read any notes, I print them out in large font and place them on a stand slightly above and behind my laptop screen. I often also use two screens, but then you have to remember the audience will see you turn your head—even if you do so only very slightly. A good ploy here is to signal your actions in advance and just say you are going to turn to read something to them.

Choose the right words.

The words you choose are vital. Choosing inclusive, active wording in story format is vital in bringing about a conversational aspect to your presentation. Words play a key role in the neuroscience of conversations and shift the neurochemistry, opening the creative parts of our brains so that we are more likely to produce higher levels of hormones such as dopamine, oxytocin, and serotonin, all of which make us feel good, positively engaged and inclusive. So, choosing the right words plays an essential part in the equation, but it is not just the words, it is also how you deliver them.

Tell stories.

Nothing helps build rapport with the audience quite like a good, relevant, well-told story, as long as it is not too long. People remember stories and find them easy to listen to. They identify with them. Stories help paint pictures in their minds and get them emotionally involved, again shifting their neurochemistry.

The opportunities for using stories are immense—you can use stories at the beginning, middle, or end of your presentation. You can keep referring to your story as you continue the presentation and develop your main message. And you can use a story format to make any example you have more interesting, i.e., set the scene and introduce the hero, describe the threat/problem the hero encounters, and explain how the hero finds the solution to the threat or problem. The audience does, of course, need to identify with the hero for it to be memorable, so make sure it really is relevant.

Use your voice—it's your most valuable tool.

Your voice is your most valuable tool for building rapport, trust, and understanding when the audience cannot see you. Make sure you keep your listeners interested by varying *speed, volume, pitch,* and *tone* naturally. Emphasise main content words and make pauses to help listeners understand what you are saying and what you mean.

It is advisable to practise this as a native speaker of the presenting language, and more so, as a non-native speaker. For example, German native speakers can sometimes sound slightly monotonous when they speak English, often because they are not used to changing pitch or making pauses much in their own language, and it can feel strange and overdramatic to them. I advise everyone to learn how to do it irrespective of whether they are going to deliver a presentation face-to-face or online.

Have you ever rehearsed your intonation and speed? Or your facial expressions? If you have not, try it. It is extremely useful and can be an absolute eye-opener, especially if you record yourself and play it back.

I've practised all of the above by doing an adaptation of an exercise I read about in *Dynamic Presentations* by Mark Powell, which can be done equally well in virtual or live, face-to-face situations. Participants are put into pairs, and each takes a text from a recent presentation they have given. If they don't have one, they can use the text of a future presentation, or you can give them a text without any punctuation. They are then asked to proceed as follows:

1. Underline the words they want to stress and mark where they want to go up or down with their voices or make pauses.
2. Read their texts to each other at different speeds and volumes, etc.
3. Read the text again, and this time, include using appropriate facial expressions that match and high-light what they are saying.
4. Deliver the text again, now also incorporating sup-porting elements of body language as mentioned earlier in the paragraph. Use your face.

In face-to-face training where everyone is present, it is easy to split the group into pairs, and the trainer can then facilitate by going from group to group. In online seminars where everyone is sitting at home in front of their screen, you can do the same thing by using breakout rooms. Of course, it is not quite the same as being physically close, but for activities such as this one, it works well.

Practice makes perfect—video record yourself presenting.

Earlier, I mentioned how we often film participants and give them feedback on their presentation skills. A real bonus of giving presentation training online is that you can video record the person presenting with the click of a button, which saves setting up the tripod and camera and transferring the data the way we often did in face-to-face seminars. Rehearsing a presentation is key, and it is just as easy for the presenters to video record themselves. They can see themselves exactly the way the audience will see them and in exactly the same setting.

There is no better way to practice! Knowing what you look and sound like gives you confidence just as much as knowing your subject inside out does.

Remember, if you have confidence in yourself, your audience will have confidence in you.

Anticipate questions.

Try to anticipate questions. Then use Zoom, Teams, Webex, or any other platform and get a friend or colleague to ask you questions so that you can practice answering them. Again—video record yourself and watch to see how confident your answers are. Make sure you speak as loudly answering questions as you did in the presentation—people often unintentionally lower their voices, which can make them sound less confident.

Visuals—create supporting slides.

Slides are there to support you, *not* to compete with you. Far too often, I see presenters competing with their slides. In those cases, I find myself trying to read everything on the slide rather than listening to the presenter. It is an absolute killer for the audience, and once the presenter has lost the audience's attention, it is difficult to win it back. Because that is when their minds start wandering. They start thinking about what they are going to have for lunch or why their boss just tried to call them, etc.

A good presentation is like a good conversation. The slides are only there to simplify, clarify, and amplify what you are talking about—your main message. So, create slides that do just that; never overload them. Your audience should get your slides within three seconds of viewing them. Also, be sure to create a lot more slides for your online presentation than you would for any face-to-face one. And maintain audience attention by going through them more quickly in a virtual situation. That way, the audience is forced to watch if they want to avoid missing anything. When people give you their attention, their brains are activated—they listen more closely, and they want to understand. So, don't muddle them with too many messages on one slide. Remember–just one idea per slide. And pictures say more than words; so, wherever you can, use pictures.

The Technology

Find out what technology you can use!

As I said, I like using Zoom. I find it very intuitive, and I have personally found it to be the most stable platform. I also very much enjoy working in HowSpace. But there are other platforms, e.g., Cisco Webex, Adobe, and of course, MS Teams, to name a few. You also need to find out what features the client has enabled. In some cases, I have not been able to use the active whiteboard because the customer had not enabled the feature for employees to use. (I got around that by using an external whiteboard—see below.) All these possibilities are now much more readily available than they were when I gave the training.

I used the following during the online seminar:

1. Breakout rooms to put the participants into groups for discussions and activities
2. Polls such as the ones below to ensure participation and break the monotony with a quiz.

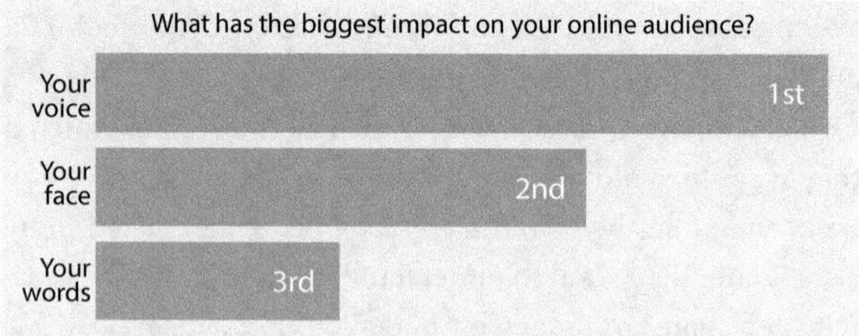

** The above shows participants' ideas, not the correct answer.*
You can also use polls to brainstorm a word cloud.

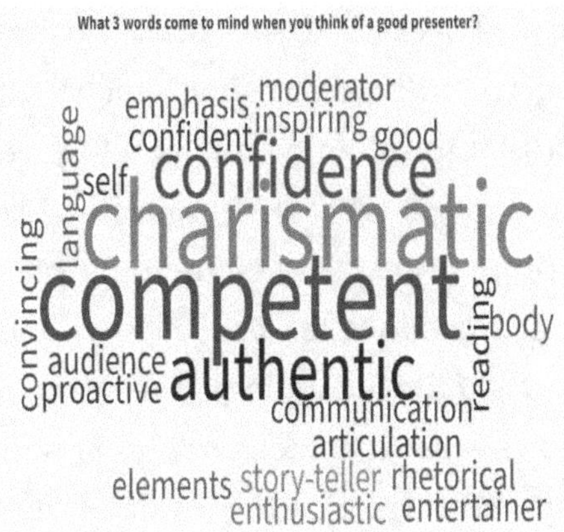

There are several options for including polls and word clouds; here, I used www.pollev.com simply because I found it easiest to integrate quickly into my PowerPoint presentation.

3. External interactive whiteboards (Jamboard and Miro). The client hadn't enabled the use of the Teams' active whiteboard. Using these, you can get the participants working together, all contributing at the same time, and you can also prepare the boards in advance so they are set up and ready to use when you need them.

4. The Chat—excellent method to quickly get people re-engaged by just asking a question and asking them to put their answer in the chat.

5. www.wonder.me—I set up a cafeteria in Wonder for everyone to have an opportunity to network. In Wonder, groups can form by themselves, just like in a normal situation after or during a coffee break. It is fun and something different.

At this point, I would like to stress how important it is that you feel very comfortable using whichever platform you have chosen or that the client wants you to work on.

You've found out everything you need to know about the audience and prepared a really compelling presentation with excellent supporting slides to keep the audience spellbound, but what happens if the technology doesn't work?

In face-to-face situations, technology is naturally important. It is always best practice to physically go to the venue and check out the microphone, loudspeakers, data projector, and presenter. Check the setting, check the room for size, and make sure you and the presentation can be seen from every angle of the room and that everyone will be able to hear you. Make sure you have a backup just in case.

And if for some reason the technology fails, you will still be present. Depending on the size of the audience, and if you have a good, strong voice, you may still be able to give the presentation with printed handouts of the presentation slides. And even if the venue is too large to do that, you may be able to find a way to stall proceedings while you get the tech up and running, e.g., by taking a break, dividing the audience into groups and giving them a task, etc.

But in an online situation—if the technology doesn't work, or if the internet fails, you fail. Technology is the most common reason online presentations fail. You have to consider that not everyone has a good, stable, and fast internet connection. So, even if you make sure your connection is good, you cannot be sure each of your participants has a good one. If the connection is too slow, showing videos becomes a problem, or people freeze mid-sentence, and you can no longer hear what they are saying.

Often, these problems are only minor, and simply shutting the PC down and rebooting will sort them out, but not always. Even if it does, it always costs time and nervous energy, and if busy people drop out, they may not return. You need to reflect and decide on how you want to react in situations like that. Will you, for example, suggest they have a cup of coffee and come back after thirty minutes the same way as you would in a live situation? And how will you do that if everything suddenly collapses? Or, if people can't access or drop out, will you ask them if you can record the session so that anyone who has a problem can watch it afterward? If so, you will have to ensure you get everyone's permission to do so.

There are no right or wrong answers to those questions. It just helps if you have a Plan B, a contingency plan of some sort, just in case.

Learning From Experience:
What went well?

1. **Creating a networking opportunity.** One of the main objectives of the course, apart from the content, was to give the participants an opportunity to get to know each other and network while learning something useful together. That was one of the main reasons it was originally set up to be face-to-face. That was also where I placed my main focus when

deciding *how* to do the various activities. Though we obviously felt we could not compare being physically together for three days at an off-site in a hotel away from the office and daily chores, being online from home for three days was, to everyone's surprise, very successful from that perspective.

2. **Working in MS Teams.** I learned to set up meetings, arrange breakout rooms, transfer documents, and was fine using all the most important features in Teams. As I predicted, I have come to use Teams for other customers as well, and as with other programs, the possibilities Teams offers continue to improve. So, for me, it was definitely useful, although the process took longer to set up than I had anticipated.

3. **Activities and method variations.** The exercises I chose for the first two days of the online seminar worked well—they were varied and interesting. Participants felt the day had flown by.

4. **Content.** Content was very relevant for this target group, and I was happy with its main focus.

5. **My presence.** During the whole seminar, I was aware that I also had to be a role model of what I was advising them to do, and the feedback I received reflected that. In other words, my slides were carefully designed; I kept my energy level high; used my face, my voice, and my hands to maintain audience attention; and I used the breakout rooms, interactive whiteboards, chat, etc. for activities at very regular intervals.

What will I do differently in the future?

1. **Adjust the timing.** The presentation lasted three consecutive days–too exhausting. Despite the fact that the seminar was highly interactive, concentration spans were quite low on the third day. I think, next time, I might try to plan to have a weekend between the second and third day. That would also give participants more time to work on their presentations and be ready to present on day three.

2. **Have two trainers, not just one.** The reason concentration was low on the third day was also partly due to content—participants delivered their twelve-minute presentations and gave each other feedback on that day. They really enjoyed this part of the seminar and found it very useful. Nevertheless, it took a long time, and irrespective of how interesting a presentation is—and even with breaks in between—after the third or fourth online presentation, concentration dwindles noticeably. With two trainers and eight participants, you can have two groups, each with one trainer in their own breakout room. That way, there would be four presentations in each group, each participant would only have to listen to three, and there would be more time for feedback and discussion afterward.

    Having two trainers can also reduce complexity in that one trainer can concentrate on looking after the technical side. So, for example, one could manage the breakout rooms, show the videos, facilitate the chat, etc., while the other leads through the actual content. This saves time, makes everything run more smoothly, and is more interesting for the participants.

3. **Plan for more time to set up and become acquainted with new technology.** I underestimated what setting up Teams would entail, which hampered my ability to efficiently manage the breakout rooms, etc., myself. I should have known, as several people had warned me, it would not be easy. I lost a lot of time when I ran into a few problems, and it took a while for me to find the right person to help me solve them. As a result, I had less time to familiarise myself with MS Teams and prepare for the actual seminar. Such issues can, of course, happen whenever you use any form of new technology.

4. **More structure.** I knew Germans love structure, and I certainly made sure I had a lot more structure than I normally do in live seminars. But I underestimated how much more you have to navigate your participants in online seminars. Everything you say has to be very explicit, crisp, and clear, and you need to say it more often than in a live in-person situation. That is because when you are physically present, you notice when someone hasn't quite understood and can react and repeat what you have said in a different way. You do not notice when you are online looking into the camera, so you have to remain very much

aware of that and plan to say things more often right from the beginning. This realisation has since helped me improve all my online communication.

5. **Less is more.** Timing is always tricky. Knowing how long activities and feedback can take is difficult to plan down to the minute in advance. As I mentioned earlier, the content I had planned was suitable and highly relevant, but we didn't get everything finished. You simply need more time to go through everything online. So, next time, I will plan for less and keep a very clear focus to make sure everything of importance gets covered adequately. I will also plan for a few extra activities to keep up my sleeve just in case we do finish earlier.

6. **Find out more about the audience.** Having always preached about how important it is to know the audience, I realised I had relied on others to give me the information I needed on the participants, and there were discrepancies that I could have avoided if I had contacted everyone individually before the seminar as I very often do. That was a very annoying mistake, and one I certainly will not be making again.

As I write these last few words, we are in the middle of the third wave of the pandemic, in total lockdown again, and I have just finished talking to a colleague who had all her contracts cancelled and has had no work for over a year. I feel for her, and I reflect on how fortunate I have been. I have been busier than ever. When the pandemic started, I, too, received emails cancelling contracts. I replied to these immediately, politely saying I fully understood and that I just wanted to let them know that if it would help them in any way, I would, and could, do all my seminars online. The response was overwhelmingly positive. They replied just as quickly as I had, withdrew their cancellations, and asked me to quote for other contracts.

I am grateful for the fact that I was in a position to react the way that I did and have been given so many opportunities where, as in this case, I was able to dive in and try things out. And I am grateful for the amazing network of wonderful coaches in the C-IQ European Collective who have so often supported me by sharing their experiences, skills, and knowledge.

Yes, I am glad I took on the challenge. I enjoyed preparing for and holding the seminar, and I discovered that a good presentation can be like a good conversation irrespective of whether it is off or online. I learned a lot along the way and now enjoy sharing those learnings with my clients, my colleagues, and last but not least, with you as my readers.

References

- Duarte, N. (2012). *HBR Guide to Persuasive Presentations.* Boston, MA: Harvard Business School Publishing Corporation.
- Powel, M. (2010). *Dynamic Presentations.* Cambridge, UK: Cambridge University Press.
- Lewis, R.D. (2006). *When Cultures Collide: Leading Across Cultures.* London, UK: Nicholas Brealey International.

5

A Multipath Process to Facilitate Online Teams to Thrive in Virtual Co-Creation Sessions

By Christian Délez

Agile Project Leader | Coach | Facilitator
Neuchâtel, Switzerland

"I know that you believe you understand what you think I said, but I'm not sure you realize that what you heard is not what I meant"
~Robert McCloskey

It is more than one year since the worldwide spread of COVID. The way we work will never be the same again. Before COVID, some people were already practicing new ways of working with online teams to co-create. I have had the opportunity before and during COVID to facilitate co-creation with online groups, which is different than in-person groups. Here is what I have learned.

The in-person co-creation approach

When a team has to decide something, one way to do so is to organise a meeting, send some information up front, and plan the decision at the meeting. This is generally perceived by organisers as efficient and inclusive; plus, it provides a sufficient amount of upfront information to give participants an idea as to the content of the meeting.

A typical decision meeting

There are some issues with this method, which are even more visible and relevant when working virtually.

The first is a lack of engagement and no real perception of how each participant feels about the subject. Several participants are quiet most of the time. A smaller number of participants speak for around 80 percent of the meeting.

Each participant has interpreted the upfront received information in a different way and understands something different.

Facilitating a virtual meeting is hard—it takes energy and practice.

Another issue is that some thoughts, insights, and information are kept under the carpet and will not be brought to the table even if these are important in helping to make the decision.

At the end, the decision is made by a small number of participants, while the others are just nodding. Some tasks to finalise the decision work is distributed to only a few participants. Another follow-up meeting is not scheduled, and everyone continues working on other tasks and projects. It is not clear which impact the decision taken at the meeting will have on people and how the impacted people will respect and follow the decision.

A better way to get great results

I propose a way to get great results with online co-creation sessions based on my experience over several years, using the background of neuroscience and Conversational Intelligence® as well as the changes in the way we work since COVID. Remote working is not new. It has been practiced with some teams for years, and there is literature about remote work and new ways of working.

However, this new way of working is now widespread and has been quickly deployed to many sectors and industries.

We first have to understand some of the differences when working remotely.

One difference is that there is no more spontaneous side at the coffee corner, in corridors, at the smoking zone, and outside on the campus. All those little conversations where you get knowledge and insights about some people, why they act that way, what others think, are gone. Another difference is the way people interact in online meetings compared to physical meetings. People are more shy, quiet, and prone to simply nod in online meetings, and this appears as a lack of engagement from the participants of the online meeting. It is also more difficult to feel the impact and the emotions of people.

The question is, "How do you handle these differences and get great results?" My answer is to make the differences explicit and handle each one with one or more ad-hoc solutions.

Create opportunities for spontaneous talk.

In the virtual working world, spontaneous talks have to be explicitly created by the people. The routine to walk by the coffee machine at 10 a.m. and meet people has to be replaced by another routine such as a morning virtual lean coffee, where every member of the team is invited and free to opt-in and opt-out each day. As people are shyer online, it helps when someone takes the role of facilitator and asks some questions to help launch ideas. Once initiated, the conversation goes on by itself. The challenge is to make everyone speak at the beginning. You can use the "Check-In" protocol [1], one of the "36 questions to fall in love" [2], or your own icebreaker or initial question.

The important point is that everyone speaks without being interrupted by the others and that more or less equivalent time is accorded to each person. It is the job of the facilitator to monitor these aspects. Human interactions go much better when everyone has a chance to speak briefly without interruption. It opens the attention part in their brain and makes them ready to engage, and it brings connection to the people present. Each team needs to find its starting routine for the opening of any kind of meeting (formal or informal). It is a good practice to change the routine from time to time and, if needed, use a different routine for formal as well as informal meetings.

Use voice calls

Something that connects people together and should be used far more often is plain old voice calls. Many of the social network applications have a call function, either with or without a camera. Here also, people are shy and afraid to call as they don't know what to speak about. One can start with a question related to work. You can ask for help for a task or for an opinion on a subject or present an idea and ask for feedback. Suddenly, the call becomes a brainstorming and learning session while at the same time providing the opportunity for participants and the presenter to bond with one another.

Participants on the voice call can capture their insights and learnings on a digital whiteboard or piece of paper. They can use it later for their own purpose or share the content with others. An easy way to share such content is to take a picture of it with a smartphone and upload it on the team social channel or the corporate shared library used by the team.

Initiate peripatetic calls

A friend of mine who currently teaches at a high school came up with a great idea during the pandemic: peripatetic calls. This name comes from Aristotle's alleged habit of walking while lecturing [3]. The term *peripatetic* is a transliteration of the ancient Greek word περιπατητικός (peripatētikós), which means "of walking" or "given to walking about." The way my friend implements a peripatetic call is that each participant activates a video call application (Zoom, Teams, etc.) on his/her mobile phone, and then goes outside in his/her area and walks around during the call with video on or off using self-facing or forward-facing camera.

Walking voice call

Having spontaneous interaction outside of the official virtual meetings of the team is essential for the social healthiness of the team. The spontaneous talks act as a primer for connection among the team members. They get to know each other and learn how each one behaves and reacts. It helps minimize the fear of engaging in a virtual meeting. Fear generates cortisol and locks down creativity. A peripatetic call, on the other hand, helps build trust among the team members, which generates oxytocin, enabling the pre-frontal cortex (executive brain) to be fully operational and in co-creation mode [4].

Create participant engagement during online meetings.

In the virtual world, some tools we use in a physical space are not available per default: whiteboard, flip chart, eye contact, feeling the emotions through body language, etc. These tools provide ways to make needed awareness visible to navigate meetings; so, we must determine a way to transport this awareness in the virtual world.

The use of such tools must be more explicit in the virtual remote working environment. A digital whiteboard, such as Mural, Miro, or Google Jamboard, should be used. There are also facilitation techniques that help participants feel the emotions and get some of the information typically obtained by eye contact when you're in the same room.

At the beginning of the meeting, the facilitator starts with the Check-In round. The facilitator role can be taken by anyone. A good practice is to change facilitators on a regular basis. After Check-In, the person owning responsibility of the agenda of the meeting presents the topic.

As people can be shy and quiet and sometimes even muted during an online meeting, the facilitator organises a question round and invites each participant by calling their name one at a time to ask a question, which gets directly answered by the topic owner. During this question round, the different viewpoints of each participant with his/her unique way of seeing the world will be clarified. This acts like a double-click on the topic.

Double-click is one of the five top conversational essentials

[5]. I came up with this concept when Judith E. Glaser noticed what happened when people working on their computers double-clicked on a folder. When they double-clicked, all of these things were inside it that they hadn't seen before or didn't remember they'd saved. Judith wondered, "What if I teach people to follow up with questions (double-click) to confirm understanding?" This is crucial because often, we assume everyone has the same understanding. Unless we double-click and confirm that we understand each other, we are just assuming that we understand, and things can quickly go awry. Double-clicking goes in deep, clarifying the meaning of the different words and sentences the topic owner used. Hearing the questions of the other participants, together with the answers of the topic owner, also brings awareness among all the participants.

It is important that this process is facilitated by one of the participants taking over the facilitator role for that meeting. He/she acts as a timekeeper, calls each participant to engage, moderates the speaking time such that everyone has a voice, and refocuses the discussion if it goes off track by bringing it back to the topic under discussion.

The discussion of the topic owner, as well as the Q&A round, should be captured by a scribe on a digital whiteboard [6]. The scribe can be any participant and is tasked with capturing the knowledge and the insights of the discussion in any way she/he feels appropriate (sentences, words, drawings, visual graphic recording). Each scribe has their own style. An example of a visual recording of a session by Dominique Ara-Zwahlen can be viewed on YouTube [7]. The rest of the meeting discussion is also recorded by the scribe such that all the knowledge and insights are captured. As the whiteboard is digital, several participants can open it and co-edit the recording too. This is an example of online co-creation during meetings.

At the appropriate time, for example, before going to the next agenda item, the scribe can share his/her desktop and present the actual state of the recording. Some amendments and editing can be made. The recording of the discussion is made available at the end of the meeting to all participants. It takes the place of what is typically referred to as "the minutes" of a meeting.

Once the topic is better defined, the main discussion can take place. Depending on the goal for the meeting topic—which may be to decide something, distribute information, or gather feedback—the discussion can be facilitated in a more relaxed way, following the flow of the conversation and just refocusing or moderating the time if necessary. At regular intervals, it is a good practice to ask if anybody else has something to say, especially when there is a pattern of just particular participants speaking while others are quiet.

A scenario that occurs, especially when decisions have to be made, is that the discussion gets emotional, there is no real agreement on decisions, and there are understanding gaps between participants. In that situation, I propose to postpone the decision to another session. To close the meeting, each participant can say one sentence on how went the meeting for him/her, without any comment from the others.

Then comes the path of virtual connections in between

virtual meeting sessions. If nothing is done until the next virtual meeting, there is a big risk to end at the same status: no decision, no agreement.

Double-click session

When there is a gap between people's points of view or understanding of a topic, a good exercise to do is the double-click. For example, persons A and B have tension during a meeting on the topic of family. In a separate session, together with one colleague playing the facilitator, they do a double-click on the word "family."

First, they can do a check-in. They take five to ten minutes in silence to draw on a digital whiteboard their view of what family means, each person on their own. They can also add a few words. The facilitator colleague guides them through the process.

After those five to ten minutes, the facilitator asks person A to present his drawing, which looks like this:

Family person A

Person A speaks and explains his/her drawing, and person B listens to understand and to connect. Person B only asks clarifying questions to fully understand and connect to the reality of person A's family definition. The facilitator verifies that the process gets respected (only clarifying questions) and refocuses the conversation if needed. The facilitator also monitors time. After a max of ten minutes, he/she has the participants switch.

Now the facilitator asks person B to present her drawing, which looks like this:

Family person B

Person B speaks and explains, and person A listens to understand and connect.

As we can guess from the two drawings, the family reality is different for persons A and B. Person A has an experience of both parents being present, time together, travel and holidays, and a secure place to be. Person B has an experience of one parent partially present because of lots of working hours, not enough money, working on her own to pay for school, and having a secure space with some friends outside of the family house.

This sort of reality gap is everywhere, including in business, regarding any kind of topic: engagement, process, leadership, values, culture, inclusion, performance. The reality gaps generate tensions in conversations and meetings. The double-click exercise in between meetings is a great way to reduce the gap and bond people together. It can be done with more than two people in a facilitated workshop format with shared digital whiteboards.

After such an exercise, each person needs time to let the learnings sink in. The next meeting on the subject that generated the tension should be planned for the next day at the earliest.

Roles in co-creation sessions

There are several roles that are useful in virtual meetings or co-creation sessions:

- topic owner
- participant
- scribe
- facilitator
- observer
- navigator (mob programming)

We've covered the scribe who takes a graphics and words recording of the meeting and sessions on a digital whiteboard that serves as the minutes of the meeting.

The facilitator makes sure everyone has a say; reframes, refocuses, and redirects if people go off-topic; and monitors the time (timekeeper). Also, when tensions occur that will not be resolved immediately, the facilitator proposes a double-click exercise and schedules it as well as moves the tension generation topic to a later date.

The observer is someone not saying anything, not actively participating in the topic; however, that person is actively observing and listening to the participants and their behaviours. The role of the observer is to share his/her observations and insights on the behaviour of the participants as well as insights related to the emotions in the virtual space; for example, "This person doesn't say anything," "This person has a tone of voice that seems angry since we spoke about topic X," "I sense we could go deeper into subject Y," "This person seems sad," or, "This person looks energized." Having someone labelling what is going on helps each participant and the team gain awareness about their team dynamics, and this awareness will improve automatically over time. The observer speaks at the end of the meeting and in the middle if the meeting is long or the observer thinks it will improve the rest of the meeting.

The participant is an active member of the conversation and co-creation taking place.

The topic owner is the person who brings the topic to be discussed. He/she presents it and welcomes the feedback and insights of the participants. For a meeting with several agenda items, there can be a different topic owner per agenda item.

The roles of scribe, facilitator, and observer can and should rotate between several people. You can try what works best for you. For example, you can introduce one role at a time and experiment with it to see how it works. These roles apply to virtual meetings and sessions and help make visible what is less visible in the virtual space, thus bringing awareness to the participants. That process in the mid- to long-term will improve the bonding between people, increase engagement, build more trust, and provide greater results.

Multipath way to great results

The multipath way to co-creation and the great results are shown in the drawing below.

It starts with the first meeting I described before, where no decision could be reached as there were too many diverged points of view. At the end of the first meeting, we have the digital graphic recording, provided by the facilitator. Maybe we also have feedback from the observer (which can be explained later in the text). With this information, the topic owner, the meeting leader, or another person can organise the first steps in the multipath way: the double-click and voice calls sessions.

The organiser chooses who participates in the double-click exercise and who will have voice calls. There are no special rules for the selection of who does what. Several participants can also do both activities. There can and should be several double-click and voice calls in parallel when there are more than five people in the first meeting.

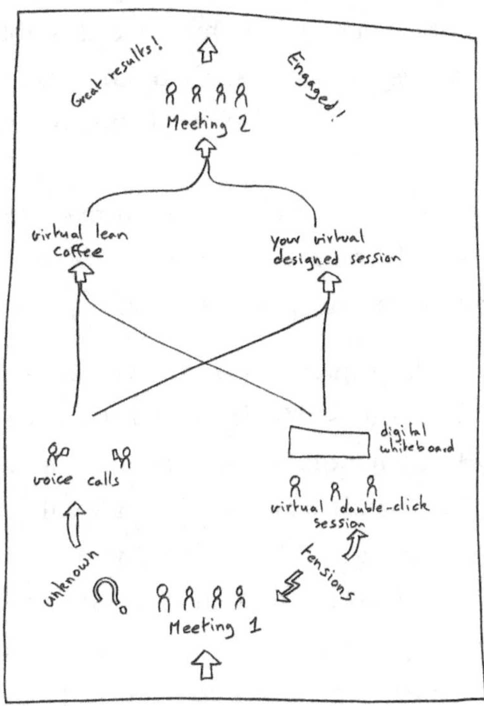

Multipath way to great results

Now comes the second step in the multipath way: the virtual lean coffee and your own virtual designed session.

The virtual lean coffee provides a format for individuals to quickly self-organize a conversation on topics that are most relevant for those who show up [8].

Your virtual designed session can take whatever form you choose; some possible methods are listed here:

- Read an article on the topic of the first meeting.
- Present a book you think will help the participants.
- Watch a TED Talk (www.ted.com) or YouTube video on the topic of meeting two.
- Go for a walk to discuss the topic. You can use the

peripatetic call way if a physical call is not possible.

- Have an asynchronous discussion thread on social media sites such as Slack or Teams or an equivalent platform.
- Host an internet search session on the topic of the first meeting and capture the learnings on a digital whiteboard.
- Offer your own idea for a session.

For step one, the organiser decides who goes to the virtual lean coffee and who goes to their own virtual designed session. Another way to do handle this step is to create timeslots and invite everyone to decide which session they will participate in.

Step three is the second meeting. Every participant had several interactions and is now more aware about the topic of the first meeting. The facilitator starts the second meeting by a check-in round in which each participant shares one thing they have learned since the first meeting. It can be on the topic, on another participant, or on something else. After the check-in round, the topic owner goes into the subject of the topic in the first meeting where they got stuck and starts a new conversation, utilizing the newly engaged and aware mindset of the participants. The facilitator helps to navigate the conversation and reframe, redirect, or refocus the conversation as needed. The flow of the second meeting is smoother than the first as every participant has had time to connect to one another as well as to gather other points of view and learning from the in-between session.

If no decision can be made, you can organise another round of step two (double-click and voice calls) and/or step three (virtual lean coffee and virtual own designed session) and go for a third meeting.

Alternative version of the multipath way

There is an alternative version of the multipath way to great results. It consists of doing only step two (double-click and voice calls) between the first and second meetings. You can even decide to do the step-two activities before the first meeting in order to prime the participants and the topic owner for the topic to be discussed and on which decision needs to be made. The alternative version could look like the figure below.

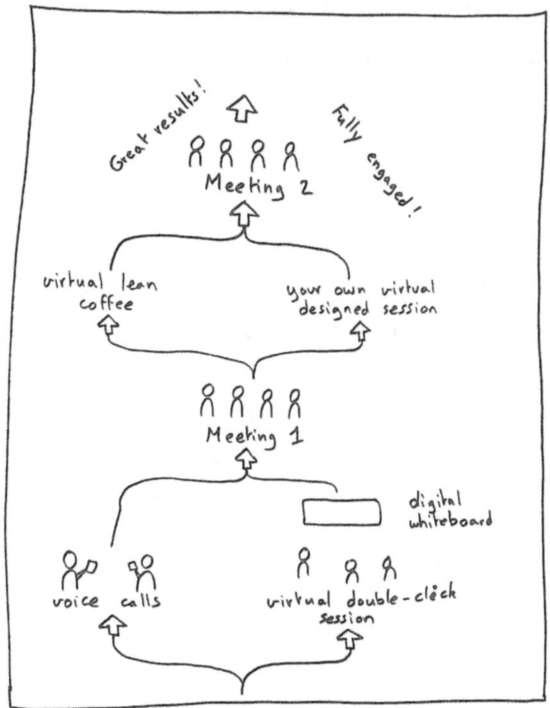

Alternative version of multipath way

The importance of (some) technological aspects

Virtual work means a high number of hours in virtual calls at home or somewhere else other than the workplace. The IT and office equipment must be adapted.

I see the biggest gains in audio, video, and the chair. A poor audio device makes it hard for people to clearly hear your message, and I experience this issue a lot in the virtual world. You don't hear how your audio device sounds as you are never on the other side of the line. Invest in a good audio hardware device.

There are good headsets. Do a test by letting someone else use your hardware while you are on the other end of the virtual call.

I want freedom of movement at my remote workplace, and I use a USB table speakerphone such as the Jabra Speak 710. It allows me to move around and keeps great sound both for me as well as any colleagues at my virtual desk (when I am in coworking spaces or somewhere else) participating in the hybrid meeting.

A comfortable ergonomic office chair is a must. It took me ten months at the beginning of the COVID pandemic of homework and back pain before I got a proper chair.

The last aspect is video. A good camera (720p or HD) provides a clear image and avoids blurry tiering images.

There are video conferencing hardware devices with video and audio integrated with only one USB cable to connect to your laptop.

My virtual hardware setup looks like the drawing below.

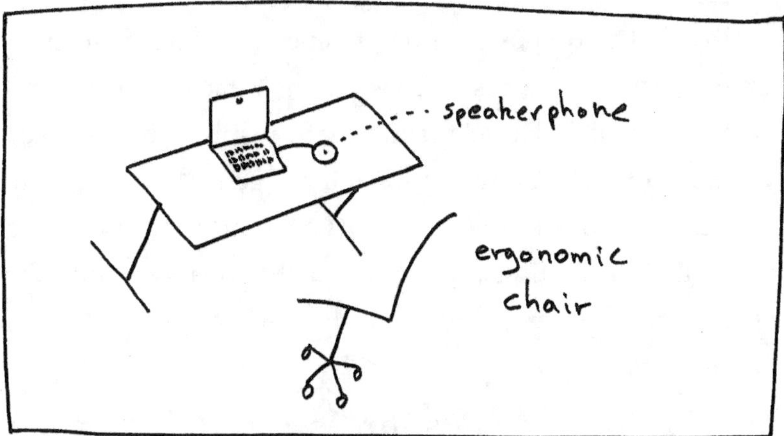

Remote workplace

I also have an extended setup for hybrid meetings with up to fifteen people in attendance at my location.

Hybrid workplace

The learnings

Hopefully, you have learned to engage an online team to co-create using practices such as having a facilitator, observers, and a scribe. These practices are inspired by remote/hybrid facilitation, Conversational Intelligence®, and years of experience. Also, we covered the asynchronous paths needed during the co-creation process to let the idea seep into the brain of each co-creator such that they bring their best at the next session.

Resources

1. "Check-In Protocol," The-Core-Protocols. Visited January 11, 2022: https://thecoreprotocols.org/protocols/checkin.html.

2. "36 Questions to Bring You Closer Together," Psychology Today, Visited January 11, 2022, https://www.psychologytoday.com/us/blog/open-gently/201310/36-questions-bring-you-closer-together.

3. "Peripatetic school," Wikipedia, Visited January 11, 2022: https://en.wikipedia.org/wiki/Peripatetic_school.

4. "The Neurochemistry of Power Conversations, Leaders who activate trust," Psychology Today, Visited January 11, 2022, https://www.psychologytoday.com/us/blog/conversational-intelligence/201701/the-neurochemistry-power-conversations.

5. Glaser, Judith E., (2016). Conversational Intelligence®: How Great Leaders Build Trust and Get Extraordinary Results, Routledge.

6. "Tools for Remote Workers," Lisette Sutherland, Collaboration Superpowers, Visited January 11, 2022, https://www.collaborationsuperpowers.com/tools.

7. "Setting Expectations, Dominique Ara, YouTube, Visited January 11, 2022, https://www.youtube.com/watch?v=UWK-EU8DPoY.

8. "Virtual Lean Coffee Chat," Mark Kilby, Visited January 11, 2022, https://www.markkilby.com/virtual-lean-coffee.

6

A Continuity or Change: A Problem or a Polarity?

By Charlotte Weston-Horsmann

Executive Coach | Intercultural Communications Specialist
Team Coaching | Leadership Development
Bernried, Germany

If you were to ask yourself today in view of our experience with COVID -19 over the past years where our focus should be now: on preventative health care or a thriving economy, what would you say? This is a very current concern, and if polarized into either/or, neither will thrive.

All too often, we chose a compromise of sorts, which often results in blinding ourselves to unaddressed concerns in an effort to maintain the balance. Blindly trying to achieve balance usually results in the opposite. Trading one concern for another risks an endless loop of compromise. A true energy-blocker! I invite you on a journey to explore a viable alternative to either/ or stuck-ness and compromise. Based on an adaptation of the Polarity Map[®1] tool, we are able to gradually surface blind spots by becoming acutely aware of the many areas of our life and work that are interlinked and interdependent.

In the example above, overfocusing on healthcare to the neglect of the economy will undermine health in the long run. Conversely, overfocus on the economy will lead to a weakened one in the long term. In other words: A healthy public is needed to support a strong economy, *and* a stable economy is needed to support a healthy public. These two poles are interdependent. Consequently, there is a very natural tension between them.

Perceiving the polarity "tension" as an either/or problem to solve can result in positional stances as sides are taken that disrupt the natural energy flow. Bringing perspective to the interconnectedness between the poles helps to leverage overfocus on one area and creates a condition that can be managed.

So how do polarities work? Mostly, we are not aware of the polarities within us in our everyday lives. Our breathing enacts a polarity as we inhale and exhale, as do our activity and rest cycles. Nature in its seasonal cycles is another prime example. Just think of the yin and yang concept of dualism in ancient Chinese philosophy. Polarities are natural energy systems that flow and interweave. Letting go of positional stances allows us to enter the flow and perceive the very natural tension that we can manage productively. In this lies the paradox: Is it a problem to solve or a polarity to manage?

1 Adapted from Barry Johnson, And: Making a Difference by Leveraging Polarity, Paradox or Dilemma: Volume 1: Foundations (Polarity Partnerships, LLC, Sacramento, 2020).

Is it a Problem or a Polarity?

We often think of polarities as problems we must solve. Problems usually have *independent* alternatives containing mutually exclusive choices and can stand alone, e.g., "Should I wear this sweater or the other one?" Here, there is one right answer, which makes the alternative "wrong."

Polarities, on the other hand, have *interdependent* alternatives. Neither pole can stand alone. There are more "right" answers that are interdependent such as with stability *and* change. Both need each other's truth as they evolve and need to be leveraged. The longer we focus on one pole to the neglect of the other, the more we get stuck in problem-thinking and a static mindset.

Take, for instance, the condition of stability and change, often also referred to as outrage and optimism that many organizations have been grappling with in the face of increased complexity and uncertainty in VUCA (volatility, uncertainty, complexity, and ambiguity) environments. Stability and change constitute a polarity, and as such, are an interrelated pair that must be leveraged to maintain a natural energy flow. When organizations, departments, or leaders unintentionally overfocus on one of the poles, the natural tension is disrupted, which strengthens the opposite pole and is experienced as resistance. Here is where an often-predictable polarity pattern emerges as complexity increases. The greater the complexity, the more important it is to be aware of the natural energy flow. This view helps to transform resistance to change into a resource for leveraging the dynamic of the poles. Gradually, the ability to leverage the polarities will increase sustainability and facilitate progress toward change.

Continuity *and* Transformation in the Brain

Think for a moment about something you enjoy doing and are really good at. You probably put a lot of energy into becoming competent at the task or activity. Eventually, you find that you can perform these without much thought as they become second nature. The brain registers these activities as familiar and integrates them into a secure base to build on. The familiar, safe foundation supports us in tackling new challenges *and* builds new skills along the way. When stress or uncertainty threatens to overwhelm us, the familiar base provides a feeling of safety. This scenario offers predictability in terms of a return on energy investment.

A frequent by-product of major change initiatives introduced into an organization is that employees can feel overwhelmed. On the one hand, a change initiative that shakes up the boredom of routine can be a welcome step outside of an employee's comfort zone. On the other, overfocusing on the change pole at the expense of the stability pole will ultimately undermine the desired change and lead to outright resistance. And herein lies the paradox: By overfocusing on the envisaged organizational change initiative without adequate attention to the stability pole, we create an energy-consuming imbalance. Both parties and the entire organization find themselves stuck in the downward spiral of what they wanted to avoid and unintentionally undermine the intended changes. By trying to avoid what we are afraid of, we end up exacerbating the polarity! In the end, both parties lose.

Working with Polarities

Recent change theories point to the importance of underlying values and beliefs that each of us have incorporated over our lifetime. Immunity to change[2], for instance, states that while striving to commit to an improvement goal, we struggle to escape what holds us back. In many cases, we are not aware that these assumptions and beliefs compete with what we really want to change in holding with our improvement goals. They keep us locked within our safe comfort zone of familiarity, for better or worse. "Competing demands" (Kegan and Lahey, 2009) describe the phenomenon in the metaphor, "one foot on the gas, the other on the brake." It is what keeps us stuck, immobile, and fear-focused.

5 Steps for Leveraging Polarities

Figure 1 below shows how we can leverage polarities in a step-by-step process: **Seeing, Mapping, Assessing, Learning, and Leveraging** (Johnson, 2020).

Figure 1: POLARITY MODEL

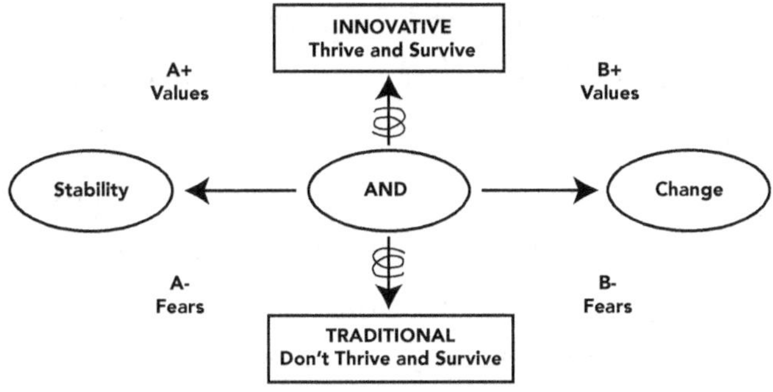

Adapted from: Johnson, Barry, AND: Making a Difference by Leveraging Polarity, Paradox or Dilemma, Volume One Foundations, (HRD Press, 2020)

2R. Kegan and L. Lahey, Immunity to Change: How To Overcome It And Unlock the Potential in Yourself And Your Organization, (Harvard Business School Publishing, 2009).

Seeing: An awareness of the interdependency factor involved is essential for leveraging the underlying polarity. Moving individuals, departments, or for that matter, whole organizations, from a traditional corporate environment (Stability) to embracing the change envisaged by CEOs is no easy task. Bookshelves are full of dos and don'ts literature that describe glorious visions and momentum, only to miss the mark in the long term. Overfocusing on the change pole to the detriment of stability leads, in many cases, to increased polarization of resistor and progress mindsets.

Mapping: Figure 1 illustrates what we need to pay attention to. It increases the clarity we need to leverage the polarities. The two poles, stability and change, are connected by *AND*. Above the center line are the values held by each of the sides (+A and +B). Below the center line are the fears that each side holds (-A and -B). As mentioned, overfocusing on one set of values at the expense of the other disrupts the natural tension between the poles, creating an imbalance that is likely to exacerbate resistance and move momentum in a downward spiral (-A and -B) toward traditional (*we don't thrive and survive*). The situation can be successfully managed by becoming acutely aware of the natural tension between values *and* fears inherent in both stability *and* change. Respecting each other's values and acknowledging fears is a first step toward leveraging the polarities and gradually moving above the center line toward the greater purpose statement (innovative, *we thrive and survive*).

Assessing: Mapping visualizes where we currently stand.

For instance, we can ask, "How close are we as an organization to moving toward an innovative organization that is equipped to survive into the future?" as opposed to the downward spiral toward remaining a traditional organization that is struggling to survive into the future. In assessing +A, I might ask myself, "How secure do I feel right now? How far can I stretch without losing the security of my comfort zone?" In +B, I could ask, "Am I agile and energized enough to take on this risky new project?" And how about minimizing the lower quadrant downside? In -A, I could ask, "Am I showing signs of slowing down due to lack of clarity?" For -B, in turn, I could ask, "Do I feel extra tension from overextending myself recently?"

Assessing our current status illustrates where we are along the middle line in terms of moving up from "We don't survive" to "We survive and thrive."

Learning: So, where is the learning from our assessment results? The assessment offers a starting point from which to embark on the greater purpose journey. You could become aware of a renewed spark of energy that is missing in your life and work. Or you could be noticing signs of overextending yourself by pushing forward too fast and a need to down-regulate. Whatever the learning, the assessment will prepare us for the next step of leveraging and moving toward a more innovative organization.

Leveraging: Steps 1 through 4 are about understanding our present situation.

Step 5: Leveraging involves putting the energy within the polarities to work to see a difference emerge. This begins with:

1. Recognizing early warning signs and self-correcting as soon as possible.
2. Taking action steps to gain and maintain momentum toward the greater purpose statement.

Case Study: Leveraging Polarities

A global biopharmaceutical company with headquarters in Atlanta, Georgia, initiated a company-wide change initiative with the goal of implementing agile production processes at all its overseas sites. Their vision was to expedite more robust and efficient manufacturing processes to remain competitive in a continually changing market environment by coordinating self-organizing teams with cross-functional expertise.

Challenges

This case follows the gradual reorganization of long-standing specialist teams in the down-streaming (manufacture of a purified protein product) process of the company's overseas subsidiary. The process involves five separate process stages prior to the final release of the product. Separate units derived from each of the five teams, consisting of approximately ten area specialists and headed by team leaders, are responsible for implementing stages 1 through 5, respectively. The team leads answer to the units' line managers who are responsible for product release in their area of specialization before it is moved on to quality control. Quality control teams for each area give the green light for final release.

Stages of down-streaming: Five specialist areas (units)

1. Fermentation units

2. Product isolation units
3. Final product processing units
4. Validation units (product readiness)
5. Verification and product readiness units (line managers)
6. Final product release (quality control)

Management levels:
- Level 1: Team leaders
- Level 2: Line managers
- Level 3: SLT quality control

Managers at their US-based headquarters were becoming increasingly dissatisfied with the top-heavy hierarchical structure, which was slowing down production time, causing bottlenecks and costly delays. They were already well underway with change initiatives at the Atlanta location and were eager to roll it out to overseas subsidiaries.

Proposed Changes

An executive team from the regional site visited headquarters in Atlanta to meet with counterparts and familiarize themselves with changes implemented there.

Upon their return, the team formulated a change strategy based on the "lean" measures that formed the core of the initiative together with the production senior leadership team. This, they believed, could be gradually implemented. Roughly, it consisted of:

1. Two kick-off meetings at the offshore site to:
   a. Develop a strategy draft on how to onboard, inform, and involve the local SLT in the change initiative

    b. Inform and involve line managers in the respective down-streaming units

2. An envisaged strategy to:

    a. Reduce the number of area specialists in each unit from 50/unit to 30

    b. by offering early-out severance packages for employees over fifty-five and requiring team members to apply for other positions within the company.

    c. Rotate remaining specialists between units (cross-functional training).

    d. Eliminate team leader function and implement agile working, e.g., accountable self-organizing specialist teams with defined responsibilities, including documentation and daily huddles.

    e. The five line managers maintain their positions as supervisors for their respective units and attend the daily huddles to remain informed about critical events and other irregularities in the specialist areas that affect both people and processes. In addition, they will be asked to attend leadership trainings for agile working, which they will convey to the specialist teams in their units.

3. What happened next?

I had been coaching one of the functional area expert teams together with their team leader, Thomas, for cross-cultural competence in preparation for their collaboration with colleagues in the US when this change initiative took hold.

Resistance to the changes was becoming almost palpable within the team. To add to the general sense of uncertainty, COVID-19 hit and was rapidly morphing into a worldwide pandemic. A considerable number of area experts had already been rotated out of their units for cross-training. Staff not directly involved in the actual production processes transitioned to working in their home offices while the remaining area experts, now reduced in number, came to the company in turns in accordance with social distancing legislation to keep production running. As an external coach, I was no longer permitted on site.

Thankfully, I was asked to continue the coaching sessions virtually. Given the added anxiety factor, I met with Thomas, who stayed with the team on an interim basis. Together with Alex, his line manager, we decided to shift focus and open a forum for addressing the fears the team was experiencing.

Changes Caused Uncertainty and Anxiety

- Employees above the age of fifty-five were offered an early-out severance package. A number of employees throughout the organization opted for this as an alternative to reapplying for other positions within the company. This was also the case in the down-streaming department, resulting in the loss of valuable expert knowledge and skill.

- A number of area expert colleagues and team leaders were given an incentive and asked to reapply for other positions within the company. This caused a considerable amount of uncertainty and anxiety as there was no guarantee of commensurate standing and pay.

- The respective teams in the functional areas had, over the years, developed ways of working together and coalesced into silos. Competitiveness exacerbated by standardized KPIs (Key Performance Indicators) standing created a lack of transparency and distrust. There was more concern about looking good on KPIs than for inter- and intra-team collaboration.

- Agile work processes were causing confusion, irritation, and anxiety about work overload with fewer resources. There was little understanding around the new approach. There was suspicion that it was "just" another management trend foisted upon them by headquarters.

- There was a cultural disconnect in that a senior leader from headquarters visited the site with the intent of getting buy-in for the change initiative. She presented the news in an overly enthusiastic way, giving examples of how well the new approach was working at headquarters. The presentation came across as too "over the top" and missed its mark entirely. The presenter showed little knowledge of the current situation at the site or particular interest in the peoples' needs.

Alex, who had initially contracted me, was open to and supportive of the idea of switching our focus to immediate concerns. With the team's okay, we invited him to visit our sessions at regular intervals.

Where the team had been managing their workload and

delivering mostly within the given timeline, they now felt stuck. Bottlenecks in the production areas caused frustration as dead-lines could not be met. Morale in the entire department had never been lower. With resistance so strong, the first thing I did (could do!) was listen as team members vented their frustration. Thomas was among the first to veer away from the negativity and see advantages to the new agile working approach. Together with a few other members, he had been noticing an atmosphere of complacency throughout the functional areas. Moreover, he was well aware of the competition among the teams that was hindering productive collaboration and progress. This "split" from others in the team who felt more comfortable holding on to the "old way" risked polarizing team members.

Uncovering Polarity Tension

This was my opening! I introduced Alex and Thomas to the Polarity Model and asked them if they thought the team would be willing to experiment with it in an effort to gain clarity around the current situation. The team trusted Thomas as they had collaborated at eye-level in the past, although

-A Early Warning Signs	-B Early Warning Signs
• Complaints about work overload and lack of resources • Speculation and rumors • Frustration over unclear roles • Increased absenteeism	• Energy bursts followed by depletion • Impatience with less rapidly paced colleagues • Overly future-focused, irritated by the resistance • Burnout due to little renewal time

they were now anxious about his imminent departure.

Alex, Thomas, and I got together for a discovery session to explore some of the Early Warning Signs that they saw emerging in both the -A and -B categories:

Further, Alex and Thomas formulated their aspiration and intent to provide a guiding framework for what they aspired to achieve together with the team. The final action plan would be co-created to include both factions within the team to make sure everyone was on board.

<table>
<tr><td>

Envisaged Action Steps +A
- Understand the value of AND thinking
- Align talent with responsibilities
- Create on-the-job learning opportunities
- Ask questions, get curious, take initiative

</td><td>

Envisaged Action Steps +B
- Understand the value of AND thinking
- Create learning and upskilling hubs
- Listen and respond to team needs
- Set up regular check-ins to monitor team temperature and preempt rising frustration levels.

</td></tr>
</table>

The next step was to surface and cluster underlying values and fears held by both factions. These would provide the building blocks for leveraging polarization. We used a team MIRO board to capture elements that were important to members under "Values" and "Fears" around the changes taking place. Posts could be kept anonymous, allowing for more freedom of expression.

The team vacillated between resisting and emerging curiosity. Once we got the teams' okay, Thomas and I, having previously gone through the 5 Steps, got together with the team to introduce the exercise.

The board allowed us to see the unspoken values and fears in the room that, if not attended to, could undermine collaboration. It also provided a snapshot of where the team stood at the moment. Keeping the "higher purpose" of "we survive and thrive" in mind, we used the Polarity Model to cluster fears and values relative to stability and change. This normalized fears by bringing them out into the open and making them okay. Taking the edge off fear in this way allowed for feelings of psychological safety, more openness, and even curiosity regarding exploring different possibilities for moving forward as a team. We playfully introduced a "piggy bank": Whenever "or" or "but" came up instead of "and," the person added a small amount to the piggy. The interaction took on a gaming characteristic while strengthening exploration and cohesion.

Once the team opened to the idea of interrelatedness in the place of polarization, the next step was to assess what needs had to be addressed in holding with the greater purpose statement both individually and as a team. One question in this respect was: "How ready am I to move toward change?" Here, the thinking evolved incrementally toward thriving and surviving and away from a focus on not thriving/surviving.

Referring back to the 5 Steps, we asked what the learning was from the assessment results. Based on the question above, we asked team members to suggest small actions steps that could underpin the learning—in other words, leveraging resistance and forward motion to move with the energy within the polarity. We also stressed the importance of addressing early warnings that could impede momentum. Gradually, we observed elements of our initially envisaged action steps beginning to emerge.

Summary

The Polarity Model provided overall clarity around the current situation. Before delving further, the team agreed on rules of engagement that included mutual respect and listening to understand rather than nurturing assumptions and jumping to conclusions. Team members learned the value of self-regulation and how to calibrate early warning signals to take a step back and reorient.

They were able to see and accept the different levels of readiness for change among team members: those who were ready and eager to act (progress mindset) and those who were not yet ready to let go of familiar patterns (resistor mindset). Whereas formerly, this situation was seen as a problem to overcome, it had now turned into a polarity to leverage, thereby minimizing the confrontational potential. The team decided that the ready-to-move forward faction would form a task force consisting of team scouts. Their role was to network and monitor the pulse of change throughout the company, bring in the new learning, and brainstorm possible areas of application in the specialist area. Team discussions became growth-oriented and focused. Despite the challenging daily workload, members became receptive to new approaches and supported each other. Increasingly, they felt heard and valued.

The teams gained more and more clarity around moving toward the higher purpose, "we survive and thrive." The leveraging polarities exercise gradually became the standard go-to tool for creating clarity around roles and purposeful action, replacing the former command-control notices posted on the team's now virtual huddle board.

This was more than any of us could have hoped for. It was an exercise in spontaneous experiential learning, and it took hold! The team set an example in how they collaborated with each other and the pace at which they were able to move the product through the pipeline with less time discussing and arguing about how things should be done. Instead, there was clarity and focus. Thomas was asked to introduce the polarity exercise to other teams in the department, meaning that instead of being rotated out of his role as team leader, he now took on the role of multiplier and facilitator. He initiated and facilitated experiential learning hubs that were backed up by senior leadership and offered to employees and senior leaders throughout the organization.

7

ANIOU™ Opportunity to (Re)Connect and Co-Create in Virtual Meetings and Beyond

By Varda Kauffmann-Trauger

Executive coaching | Team coaching
Embodied and Mindful Leadership | Facilitator | Speaker
Zikhron Ya'akov, Israel

"The pandemic accentuated that to survive, we must (re)define and (re)find our connectedness: A positive and healthy connectedness that creates a dynamic balance between everyone's individual needs and the collective's needs."

The pandemic has caused collective fear and massive changes that (re)formulate how we live and work together. It has impacted our social connectedness. To survive, we had to go against our fundamental human instincts and socially distance ourselves, sometimes even from our loved ones. Instead of feeling safe with others, we began to perceive almost anyone as a potential foe. Although to overcome such a crisis, we need to trust each other and walk hand in hand—respecting our differences and eventually agreeing to make the best possible decisions in uncertainty—it seemed we were splitting apart.

When we use the word "WE," we usually refer to a group of people that we have something in common with. This WE acknowledges the individuals only as long as they belong to the WE group but ignores the individual's needs, specificity, and uniqueness. And in opposition, we see an I-centered trend that has lost the sense of WE. The "WE" has shifted. We are no longer able or willing to be part of an old WE. And the "only me and for myself" culture is also leading us nowhere at best, and at the worst, to catastrophe.

The pandemic accentuated that to survive, we must (re) define and (re)find our connectedness: a positive and healthy connectedness that creates a dynamic balance between every-one's individual needs and the collective's needs. Although we live in distinct bodies, we are interconnected, and we influence each other for good or bad. To survive, grow, and blossom, we need to aim at this balance. There is no perfect balance, but a never-ending inner and inter-play of balances.

ANIOU™ compass to navigating together in our fast-changing world

To get to this redefined connectedness, we need to define it together and use a compass to reach it. ANIOU is a new word that defines the way to reconcile the differences by mak-ing them visible, acknowledging them, respecting them, and creating something new together that gives place to everyone.

ANIOU is a compound word of two Hebrew words for I and We (in Hebrew, *"Ani"* and *"Anou"*). It also reflects the core ideas: In English, you may phonetically hear the words "Anew" and "an(d) you" that refer to being *together* and listening to each other harmoniously in *a new way* and with fresh eyes. ANIOU is not just something you talk about but an embodied aspiration, a state of being and doing. ANIOU is the ultimate and healthy linkage of the distinctiveness of every person into a whole that is bigger than the sum of its parts. A whole that does not hide or negate individuality. On the contrary, it grows both the WE and the I. But do not confuse it with ease and comfort. At times, it might demand effort and discomfort.

Imagine each of us being a small sun spreading our yellow light around us—we ALL shine; Our WE is blue, like water—these are our common goals, experiences, history. We are social beings in need of connectedness. Our need for social connections, says Mathew Liberman, is the bedrock upon which all other needs, such as food and shelter, are built.[1] And when the many individuals meet their social needs—the yellow and the blue merge into green—they grow and develop to be ANIOU. This ANIOU is neither permanent nor stable.

Sometimes it is bluer; sometimes it has more yellow. But at any given moment, it doesn't erase the individual's needs or voices. And sometimes, we may be out of it, but just in the blue or in the yellow part.

Why ANIOU? Because you need to know where you are and where you want to go in order to get there. Having a word to designate our shared destination enables us to make sure we get there, or at least head in the right direction.

I have been using ANIOU as a compass explicitly and often implicitly. It's a way of making the invisible visible, detecting where things are imbalanced. It is the integration of many theories and practices of which the core foundations are: the understanding that the source of ANIOU is in nature, in our body, and in our relationships[2]; and the ways to develop and strengthen it until it becomes deeply embedded and embodied in ourselves and in our cultures, are through Conversational Intelligence® (C-IQ)[3], mindfulness, and embodied awareness.

Video conferencing

To overcome the limitations and physical distancing caused by COVID-19, many people and organisations adopted new technologies and significantly increased their use of digital and virtual means of communication.

Among these technologies, video conferencing[4] has become widely used. What was once a "nice to have" and mostly used by global corporations, became one of the key technologies used for working together in teams and with groups during the COVID-19 pandemic[5]. They offered a solution for bridging distances, saving travel time, and offering more time flexibility, to name a few.

Meeting synchronously in a video conferencing space (i.e., Zoom room) is different in many ways from meeting in the same physical space. Many books and articles give suggestions about the best way to conduct effective digital meetings, engage employees in virtual teams, and create trust. Surprisingly, there isn't much research about the way video conferencing affects us psychologically and physiologically, especially since it has become so widely used for so many hours at a time and by larger numbers of people[6].

For over a decade, meeting virtually offered me the opportunity to coach clients, facilitate groups, and learn from teachers I would have probably had little chance to learn from otherwise,[7] not to mention meeting new people from around the world.

Video conferencing allowed me to join the C-IQ European Collective[8]. In September 2020, because of the pandemic, we held the online event "Changing Conversation for a Changing World" for managers. It was during this event that I co-facilitated with Tanja Murphy-Ilibasic the online workshop "Priming for Changing Conversations" for about forty participants. It was an experiential and insightful workshop that received positive feedback. I would like to share a small personal moment that I experienced during this workshop.

I had been used to working online with small groups, where I could see everyone on the same screen. Because this workshop was larger, I could see only a part of the audience at once. They looked so small on my screen, I couldn't see their expressions or fully sense their presence. Were they following me? I couldn't even see my co-presenter, Tanja. I had to guess many things. While I was presenting, I had to assume participants were listening and engaged and rely on my partner to tell me if something needed more attention or explanation. I was online with many people but alone in my office.

That was my experience. I began to wonder what experiences others were having. In the following month, I explored and analysed the virtual meetings I participated in—as a facilitator, leader, or participant.

Before I share the practices I have adopted, I would like you to explore for yourself how you personally experience meetings in virtual spaces—especially in the context of teams and groups—as much as possible through your senses and emotions.

Be true to yourself. Where are you right now? Are you sceptical toward this exploration? Maybe you are even reluctant to try and think it is a waste of time and will jump ahead to the conclusions. Are you waiting to see what comes up? Surely, some of the things you are about to be asked to notice or question, you have already noticed. Or are you willing to be curious? Are you willing to put aside what you already know and discover it anew? Let's begin.

How do you experience virtual meetings?

Read the following and imagine the experience you would be having while participating in a virtual meeting with a few people, your team, your board, or a group of colleagues. As you read, tune in and connect with all your senses. Try at first to envision a situation you are quite comfortable in.

Remember: Focus as much as you can on your senses and less on cognitive observations.

You are sitting on your chair in front of your computer. You're just about to click the join meeting button. Try to sense your body, your posture. Do not try to give words to your sensations, just notice, feel! No judgment; there is no good nor bad—it is what it is!

- [Take the time you need between the questions.]
- How are you sitting? What is your posture?
- Are you relatively upright, stiff, relaxed, or even droopy and slack?
- Sense your breathing, its rhythm and depth. Do not try to change it!
- Where in your body do you feel it is cool? Where do you feel warmth?
- Do you feel any pressure, heaviness, or tightness anywhere in your body?
- Is there a place where you feel openness or lightness?
- Do you feel an overall stillness or, on the contrary, movement and outgoing energy?
- What else do you notice about yourself, your sensations?
- Now sense the room around you, the light, the colours, the temperature. Is the temperature right for you? Is it quiet or noisy?
- Does the room feel spacey or crowded? Big or small?
- Anything else you notice?

[imagine] You are now joining the virtual meeting.

Each participant is in a separate space, somewhere. Each of them is in a separate rectangle on your screen.

- Do you choose to see the speaker in large-scale (also called "speaker view"), or do you view all your team at once (in "gallery view")?

- How do you feel now? Has anything shifted in your sensations?
- What portion of their body do you see?
- Is the quality of their images or the lighting good enough to notice their facial expressions? Their body postures?
- What can you sense about them? Their mood, their posture? Can you sense some of the things you had sensed in yourself? In your environment?
- What other things can you notice about each of the participants–their mood, attention, energy, engagement?
- What can you guess? What things are you curious about?
- Can you see their eyes? What are they looking at?
- Are you seeing yourself too?

Take a deep breath and see what these sensations tell us.

[If you wish to capture those sensations, now you can write them down.]

Remember, there is no judgment, not of anyone's sensations nor of the virtual meetings. There are many advantages to virtual meetings. Can you think of the way you benefit from them? How about your colleagues or employees? How can they benefit from this type of meeting?

What are the distinctive characteristics of the virtual meeting experience?

Let's explore some aspects that might influence our perceptions and sensations during a virtual meeting.

We have no possibility to influence or help improve each other's physical conditions—temperature, environmental noise, distractions, light. We can neither help nor disturb each other. I cannot offer you a coffee, and you cannot ask my neighbour to lower the volume of their music (especially as it might be one of my family members).

I have a *very limited way to control* the way I appear on your computer or how you hear me. You may reduce my frame or watch the whole group in gallery view—seeing everyone in small, thumbnail pictures—or enlarge the speaker to fill in the screen at the expense of not seeing the others' full expressions. You may even mute the volume on your side, and I wouldn't even know.

Uncomfortable eye gaze: If you are not looking straight at the camera lens, we lose the feeling of eye contact. And since the camera is usually set above the screen, in most cases, I can look at the camera or at the screen; either way, one advantage comes at the expense of the other. Moreover, we have no way of knowing at which participant the other participants are looking, so we might feel some discomfort because we sense we are either being watched all the time or not being seen at all.

Hard to see body cues or facial expressions. We see only a small portion of our conversation partners, and the more participants you have in a meeting, the less it is possible to see all of them on the screen at the same time. When you enlarge the speaker's picture, you can hardly perceive the others. Since we cannot perceive each other's body cues accurately, the bigger the group, the harder it is to know who wants to talk next.

Loss of a certain sense of spontaneity. We cannot pop into our colleague's office for a small question or have a chat at the coffee corner. Leaving the virtual meeting is abrupt, and once we leave it, everyone is back in their own isolated space.

A gap between the perception of oneself and of those on the screen. Does my perception of myself change because although I meet with real people in real-time, they appear on my screen smaller than in my physical reality? In addition, does the size of the frames of the participants impact how we perceive them? Does their localization on the screen impact how we perceive them? We are not around a table.

What can research tell us about meeting virtually?

From the day we are born, we learn to connect and interact physically. Video conferencing is a different way of connecting and is probably here to stay. There is increased attention given to what is named "Zoom fatigue" and to the possible causes[9], including: Eye gaze at a close distance looks very realistic but not socially realistic—we cannot tell at whom a participant is looking; cognitive load because participants need to work harder to send and receive [especially nonverbal] signals and interpret them; reduced mobility; and an all-day mirror[10]. So, how do virtual meetings really impact us in the long run— our personal well-being, our relations and relationships, and our work together?

It will be a while before research can provide us with scientific answers. But we are already working virtually and need solutions to make our work more productive and less stressful. Our nervous system is constantly looking for signs of danger[11], and only when we can mitigate the fear and feel safe can we start to build trust; work together and co-create; find solutions, especially creative ones; and plan for the long term. Not only are we living in a period of fear of physical threat and uncertainty but video conferencing also seems to increase the amount of uncertainty and fear because of the things we cannot see, hear, or control and the way our senses are impacted.

We use our entire bodies to make sense of other people. We understand others by "answering" ourselves unconsciously: "How would I feel if I did the same movement that I see the other person is doing?" And it is the same neural networks that we use to make an action that help us figure out and understand another person's perceptions, intentions, and actions[12]. Linguistic and visual cues influence our physiological synchrony and the way we correctly interpret the thoughts and feelings of others[13].

Our senses—those that help us sense our own body (interoception), our body's movement and position (proprioception), and the exterior world (our five senses, exteroception)—are all significantly impacted when we communicate and work together in the virtual space. Hence, our senses may be slower to capture information, and we might misinterpret things or miss cues coming from ourselves or from the people we meet with.

We can overcome these changes but only by making them visible and by addressing them explicitly—to ourselves and with the people we meet virtually. We need to become aware of them and take control back into our hands by learning how to use video conferencing adequately. Now that we realise what is different, we have *made the invisible visible*, and we can deal with it and try to look for new and hopefully better ways to do these things.

How to (re)gain our ANIOU

Based on the scientific research and real-life practices, there are approaches and practices that can bring more synchronicity to video conferencing meetings. ANIOU makes these practices even more powerful.

Keep in mind the ANIOU COMPASS(ion)—this compass directs us toward more integrated individuals and society. This includes teams and organizations. Integrated means linking the different parts without losing the distinctiveness of each, for example, our internal and our relational being, or linking the people into a team without losing their individuality.

The COMPASS of video meetings makes sure we use this technology in a way that respects the human needs of each uniquely individual participant—their needs and fears as well as their aspirations and talents—in balance with the team's goals to achieve a shared success, a balance that allows for better results but not at the expense of people's well-being.

ANIOU practices acknowledge and value the differences and then tries to link people into ANIOU teams by inviting everyone in. Here are some game-changing ANIOU practices:

Make the invisible visible. Make things visible, tangible, and actionable.

- **Share and talk about** what has changed for participants in virtual meetings, what each of them likes about these changes, and what causes them problems or anxiety. By sharing, you will be able to lower their fear and anxiety. Do not assume that what is visible to you is visible to others, and vice versa.

- **Raise awareness** of the changes to yourself and to others. Don't dismiss perspectives or feelings; try instead to co-create solutions. Raise cognitive and embodied awareness.

- **Check the pulse of your team and team members often**. Because we are missing so many cues in virtual meetings, it is important to make it a habit. It can be a simple check-in question at the beginning of a meeting and another one at the end of a meeting. Because it is difficult to perceive some cues, ask gently. Don't stay with your impressions. "Double-click"[14] to understand. Remember, your appearance in video conferencing is incomplete and therefore can be misleading or misinterpreted.

Raise and practice awareness and embodied synchrony

Practice *embodied awareness, centering, and synchronised movements together* with your team. There is much research about the benefits of mindfulness exercises in the workplaces in lowering stress and increasing productivity and performance. I found that doing short practices—between three to ten minutes long—during virtual meetings served to increase the synchrony of the group, along with their trust and willingness to share. As a result, there was less groupthink and more listening to each other during these meetings.

Moreover, by sensing what happens inside of us, we can choose how to respond (instead of reacting) and to sense others more accurately and develop more empathy and compassion toward them, even if we meet them only in a virtual space. We can (re)shape our shared space, our conversations, and our successes.

Practicing embodiment is also a good way to resource ourselves and regain our sense of our own bodies. And since we perceive others through our own body, first we need to check ourselves.

Cultivate together an ANIOU mindset to grow together

Adopt curiosity and compassion. Acknowledge that you have "questions for which you have no answer[15]." Meeting virtually is different from what we have been used to. Discover what is different for you. What difficulties might arise for you, and what do you need? What is easier for you, and how can you benefit others?

Acknowledge that it might be difficult for others but not necessarily in the same way it is for you! Be curious, not judgmental. Recognise and value differences.

ANIOUmeter. To keep track and maintain awareness, ask yourself and your team often to reveal where you are and where you want to be. What kind of balance between the I and the WE are we at right now?

In virtual meetings, we want to check how each participant feels, how safe each of us feels, and how it affects the WE flow.

- Am I getting what I need? Can I sense and am I aware of the other's needs?
- Are we giving too much or too little attention to the individual's needs or wants?
- Are we giving too much or too little attention to the group's needs or wants? Are we missing a shared aspiration? Are we in sync or not?
- What is working and what isn't?
- Are we achieving our goals–both ANIOU goals and aspirational goals as much as we are our team's and businesses' goals and results?

Inspiring Lesson

How would you react if you discovered halfway through a process that your team is not at all aligned with you? You have planned something great, or so you thought until that moment. But they don't really want to do it. They have other plans or another way of seeing or doing it.

This is exactly what happened to me in a leadership training I co-created with my enthusiastic friend, Karin Ulfhielm. It happened during the fifth session of our six-session online training for managers. Trust had built up throughout the sessions amongst the managers and with us. This training was designed to be co-creative and experiential, a laboratory for trying out together what was learned as closely as possible to their experience with their teams. To increase this effect, we had planned a mini-project in which the participants would co-create to capture all their learning, experiences, insights, and application, both individually and as a group.

Because this training was conducted virtually, we integrated the practices mentioned before to enable the managers to build trust, connection, and engagement. We checked the pulse often to allow them to raise their own awareness of where they were, share it, and understand where the rest of the group was. From time to time, we also did short digital polls, with one to two questions. Polls allow people to respond truthfully when they are not ready to give straightforward input, and while answering a poll, we are not influenced directly by how others are responding. Polls also give a visual map of the group pulse on the spot, a record to return to that can also open a discussion.

On that day, we conducted two short polls asking the participants to rate how committed they were to co-creating this mini-project and how they rated the trust in the group. The responses were clear: Most of the group was not interested in doing this project. However, it took us another exercise and about half an hour to realise what had been said "loudly" in the poll. It is hard to admit you did not expect a certain response. But we did!

We showed up vulnerable and genuinely curious to open a discussion. The trust that had built up allowed the managers to be bold and share what they didn't want and what they truly needed and wanted. We came out of groupthink to co-create with the group a special continuance program that continues to be an adventurous journey of exploration, experimentation, and co-creation. A source of knowledge and support.

Epilogue: share ANIOU way

I hope these practices will help you benefit from virtual meetings that are less stressful and more productive, effective, and human. The global pandemic and the digital changes it caused gave us the opportunity to practice adaptation to such changes. Virtual conferencing is an important example, and you can take this approach to any new challenge. If you choose ANIOU way to see each other and interact, then ANIOU (we) have a chance to make our teams work smarter and make our world better.

Notes and Resources:

1. Lieberman, Matthew D. (2013). *Social: Why Our Brains Are Wired to Connect*. Crown/Archetype. P.42.
2. IPNB—InterPersonal Neurobiology, a term coined by Daniel J. Siegel, to define a consilient field that embraces all branches of science to explore the ways in which relationships and the brain interact to shape our mental lives: from society (interpersonal) to synapses (neurobiology).
    In: Siegel, Daniel J. (2020). *The Developing Mind, Third Edition*. Guilford Publications.
3. Conversational Intelligence® was coined by Judith E. Glaser to denote the intelligence hardwired into every human being to enable us to navigate successfully with others and build trust and partnerships to create and transform our societies. Its premise is: "To get to the next level of greatness depends on the quality of our culture, which depends on the quality of our

relationships, which depends on the quality of our conversations. Everything happens through conversations."
In: Glaser, Judith E. (2014). *Conversational Intelligence: How Great Leaders Build Trust and Get Extraordinary Results.* Bibliomotion Inc. p.XV.

4. Meetings via web conferencing systems, such as Zoom, Microsoft Teams, or Cisco WebEx, just to name a few popular platforms.

5. There is a lot of data accumulating on the increased usage of web conferencing during the pandemic as well as forecasts that it is here to stay, including reports of web conferencing companies as well as big corporations and government agencies.

6. Porges, Stephen W. (2020). "The Covid-19 Pandemic is a Paradoxical Challenge to Our Nervous System: A Polyvagal Perspective." *Clinical Neuropsychiatry* 17,2, pp. 135—138.

7. Namely, the late Judith E. Glaser who brought to the world the so-needed Conversational Intelligence®; her joyful spirit, Daniel Siegel, for his InterPersonal Neurobiology; and Amanda Blake with her "Embright".

8. C-IQ European Collective is a global forum of experienced managers, leaders, trainers, facilitators, and coaches, all C-IQ certified, who work around the globe (ignited in Europe).

9. Fauville, G., M. Luo, A.C.M. Queiroz, J.N. Bailenson, J. Hancock (2021, August–December). "Zoom Exhaustion & Fatigue Scale." *Computer in Human Behavior Reports.* Vol. 4, 100119.

10. Bailenson, J.N. (2021). "Nonverbal Overload: A Theoretical Argument for the Causes of Zoom Fatigue." *Technology, Mind, and Behavior.* 2(1). https://doi.org/10.1037/tmb0000030.

11. Porges, Stephen W. (2017). *The Pocket Guide to the Polyvagal Theory: The Transformative Power of Feeling Safe.* New York: WW Norton. pp. 33–51.

12. Blake, Amanda (2018). *Your Body is Your Brain.* Trokay Press, p. 189.

13. Jospe K., Genzer S., Klein Selle N., Ong D., Zaki J., Perry A. (2020 November). "The contribution of linguistic and visual cues to physiological synchrony and empathic accuracy." *Cortex*, Vol. 132, pp. 296–308.

14. "Double-Click" is an expression coined by Judith E. Glaser that refers "to the process that mimics opening folders on your computer to drill down into details. Double-clicking enables each person to unlock the deeper connections she is making that others may not." In: Glaser, Judith (2014): p. 138.
15. Judith E. Glaser (2014). p.66.

8

A Unique Web-Based Tool for Ranking Personal Values

By Carina Vinberg

Leadership Trainer | Group Developer | Coach
Stockholm, Sweden

"People who have knowledge of and have insight into their own personal values are more committed and motivated—both in their personal lives and at work.
Living your values makes life meaningful."

The pandemic has increased our desire for collaboration and the need to connect and do things together. This desire for a unifying force that shows where we are going is something our future workplaces, leaders, and co-workers need to respond to. However, the dramatic changes resulting from the pandemic have also contributed to changes in values, both individual and collective. For many years in my coaching practice, I have used a web-based tool,

Value.Online, for ranking personal values. The process helps to get people working together in a committed and motivated way–both in their personal lives and at work, where trust and conversations are fundamental. The pandemic shifts in beliefs and attitudes make this tool even more useful.

Value.Online, as the name implies, is a unique interactive web-based tool for ranking personal values. The tool was developed by Point of Value in Lund, Sweden over twenty years ago and has been in use ever since. Value.Online is not a test or an analysis. There are three steps in the Value Basic Process. In Step 1, the user ranks what is most important to them. Step 2 is the generation of the map that provides an overview of which values are most important and which are important right now. This is used to increase insight into personal values, which is followed by Step 3: Act. Through my coaching practice, Framgångare, we have successfully used Value.Online with our clients for many years. Before I get into more depth about the tool, let's start with some basics.

What are values?

Values are at the heart of who we are, and that goes for both individuals and organisations. Values are not visible but are reflected in our attitudes, priorities, and behaviours. They influence our daily decisions and actions. There are different ways of understanding values. Point of Value makes a distinction between normative and personal values.

Normative values are the often-unwritten rules and agreements we have in families and in society that allow us to fit in and be accepted, while personal values tell us what is important, what drives us, what we dream of. These personal values evolve and change throughout our life. Everyone has approximately twenty to fifty personal core values throughout their life. These core values constitute our personal value system, a kind of dynamic constellation of core values, which often remain stable after the age of twenty.

At any given moment, there are about five to ten prioritized values that are particularly important for the decisions and choices we make. These personal core values change and evolve as a result of significant life experiences, such as changes in the workplace, illness, death, love, and existential issues.

As mentioned, values are shaped by our experiences and grow with our maturity and development as human beings.

Why is ranking important?

Ranking is about placing things in order of priority, and that is what you do with Point of Value's interactive tool, Value.Online. When you rank, two to four different values are set against each other, and you decide what is most important right now. These choices between the value words reflect how, on a daily basis, we weigh different values against each other. For example, when you listen to a lecturer, you might weigh: *Should I interrupt with a question or*

make a note of this or that? I have already heard that—should I mention it? We weigh what is most important, and by doing so, we weigh different values against each other.

Why is mapping important?

The results of the rankings are presented using maps and graphs. There are several Point of Value maps. One is the Meaning Map, and the other is the Congruence Map. The values that are ranked the highest are placed in the top field of the Meaning Map, called "Core Values."

The cycles in the Meaning Map represent three overall stages of development:

- *Cycle 1: Foundation.* This cycle illustrates basic needs for survival and a period of life when we create and re-create our identity. These values or needs, such as safety and affection, may be prioritised.

- *Cycle 2: Focus.* This cycle illustrates a time in our life when we practice and develop our identity. Values in this cycle are the criteria for everyday decisions such as fair, calm, perform, honest, knowledgeable, etc. These values are approaches, ways of being that can also be strategies to attain the values that motivate and inspire us.

- *Cycle 3: Vision.* This cycle deals with the values of our visions and illustrates what we are striving for, what motivates and inspires us to continue to evolve. These are often more complex values such as integrate and transform.

The Meaning Map

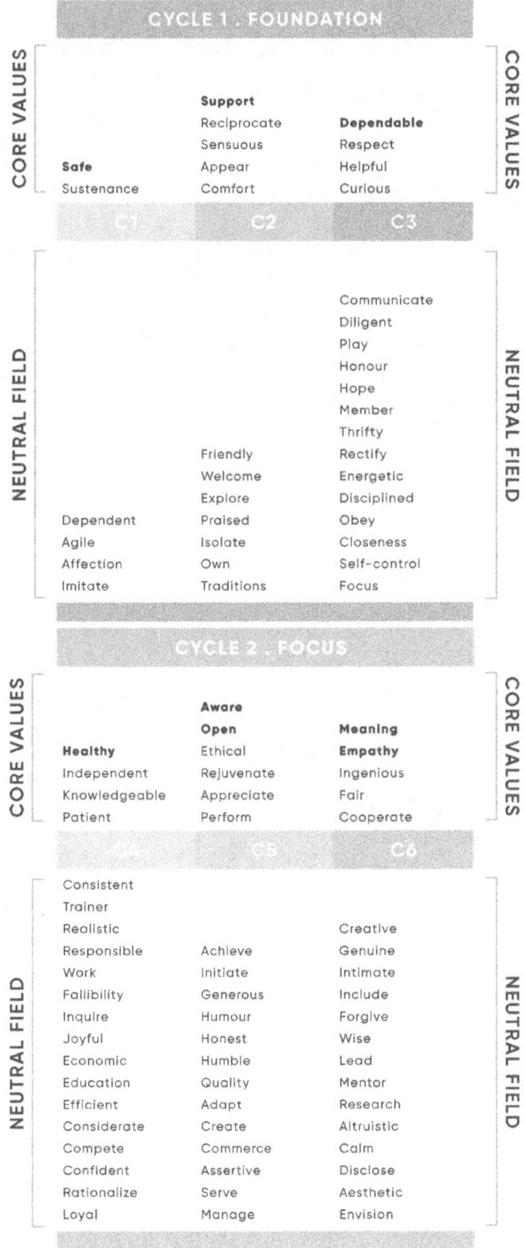

The Meaning Map

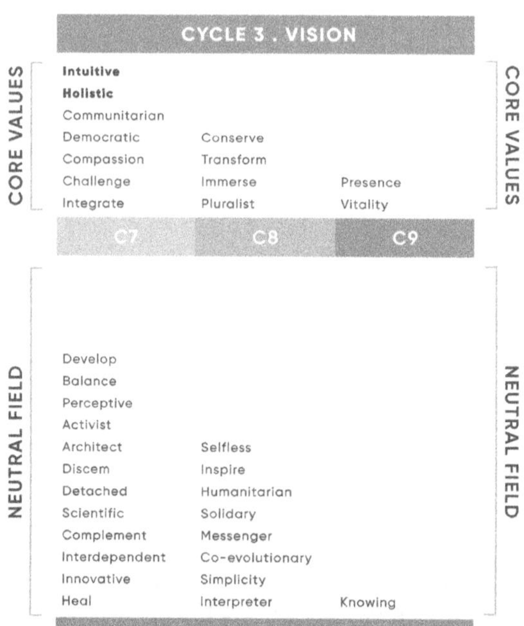

How Mapping leads to storytelling and conversations

The online ranking is a starting point for conversations with the purpose of creating insight, trust, and confidence. You rank what is important, and this generates an overview map of which values are most important and imperative, which are the driving forces and commitments that govern our priorities and actions.

When the ranking is done, the participants work together with a trained Point of Value facilitator to map out the values. Using the Meaning Map generated by the ranking, the facilitator and participants engage in a conversation about what lies behind the values. The mapping places great emphasis on the values that the individual wants to see more of and how the individual and the group can act to put more of these values into practice. An authentic dialogue is based on the premise that every person needs to be heard and understood for who they are.

How knowledge and insight lead to congruence

Several surveys show that people who have knowledge of and insight into their own personal values are more committed and motivated—both in their personal lives and at work. Studies by Barry Z. Posner and others show that increased insight and understanding of our own values is the single biggest contributing factor to increased work commitment and motivation and to a reduction in work-related stress. In addition, if people can find coherence between their own values and their workplace values, the impact is even bigger. Work-related stress and anxiety decrease. Leaders who have insight into both their personal values and the values of their organisation are perceived as more credible and find it easier to make decisions.

In order to achieve congruence between the individual and the organisation, an intermediate, vital step is needed. Extensive studies show that this step is about trust and communication.

In this step, the team formulates and adopts common values and deliberately creates an organisational culture that harmonises with the objectives and aims of the organisation. In this way, you can increase coherence and create a positive working culture where the individual thrives, the team performs, and the organisation is successful. The team culture is made up of the common behaviours and priorities that the team stands for and which the group practices.

How the Congruence Map is structured and used

The order of values is divided into four groups that represent the basic conditions for creating trust and communication between people.

Relational values are values we want to practice to create meaningful relationships. They describe the relational style and relationship environment that are important for practicing our personal values.

"Being values" (ethical-social values) are values that represent how we think we should prioritise and how to behave in interpersonal relationships, partnerships, and teams to make things work well.

"Doing values" (economic-pragmatic values) focus on performance, efficiency, and the structure we think is needed for groups and partnerships to really accomplish something that is both practical and valuable.

"Role values" illustrate the initiatives, roles, functions, or vocation that we like to have or take on in groups and collaborations.

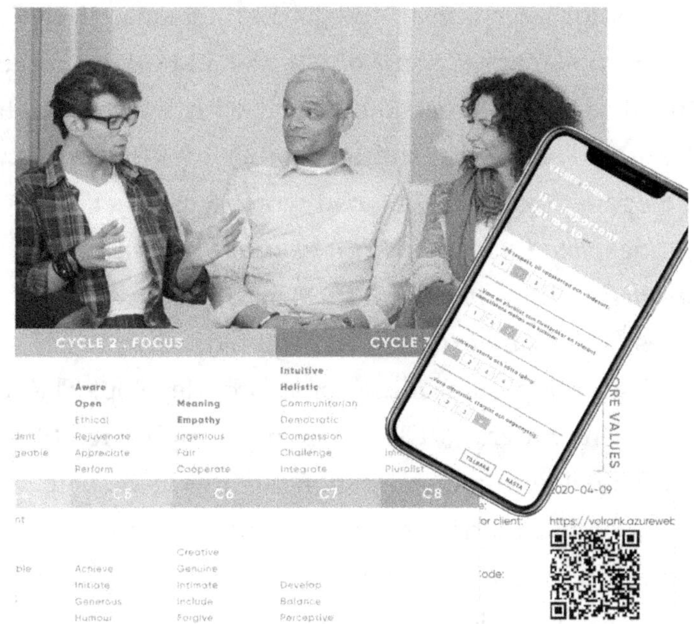

Case Histories: Working with values

We have found it very powerful to work with values in different settings, including management teams, leadership training programs, and individuals.

The following case studies show a variety of different possibilities and outcomes. See them as inspiration for you and your company and/or team. This is one way to investigate how each of us in this changing world can become more efficient together and build trust for a sustainable future.

Case History #1: How a management team used the Value.Online tool

The managing director of Hydac in Sweden wanted to use the tool for his team in a development program that was in process for over a year. By sharing personal stories and stories from managers, some of whom had been on the team for twenty years, a great foundation with which to tighten the team and to understand each other was formed. It was an eye-opener for those who had worked together for a very long time. *Now I understand why you act like that…. I have an understanding of you now that I know more about you.*

These words are from the managing director:

"A leadership team must constantly develop. The team development program, Clear, Confident and Credible, has been a valuable vitamin injection for my leadership team. The program was carried out with a big presence. The down-to-earth style of the facilitator mirrors how the participants dared to go into a deeper and more personal dialogue with each other during the time of the program. There was enough time for reflection in between the sessions, which is important, as a leadership team often has a full calendar.

Personally, I have gotten a better insight into myself as a leader. Many interesting conversations were held around values and behaviours, which are important, I think, to reflect upon and around to strengthen yourself as a leader and a manager. The program also included a coaching module where individual action plans were discussed.

I can warmly recommend this if you are looking for a leadership development program where focus lies within strengthening every individual´s credibility as a leader and manager. Especially if the group is newly put together. The positive attitude of the facilitator also makes the program easy to digest. Even if parts might seem heavy, I was looking forward to every workshop. The program was very good for my leadership team, and all members have become closer to each other since we now know each other better. It is as simple as that!"

A few years later, the managing director chose to work with Framgångare and the Value Based Processes once more with his new, updated management team, which had some newly recruited younger team members. This time, the goal was to strengthen the position of the Swedish subsidiary on the Nordic market. This program also included a WHY process to discover the mission of the company, a powerful process that was fast and successful as it built upon the foundation created during the individual Value processes.

Case History #2: Using the Value.Online tool in a leadership training program

This is an excellent tool to use in leadership programs. We used this in an open program offered to leaders within the Construction Sector in Sweden. For most participants in this program, this was the first time they realized and got into a deeper level of understanding of what drives us—our cultural differences and how most people do not know or differentiate between personal values and values of the organization. As the program evolved, they developed as individuals and leaders.

This is what participants said:

- "I got a very good insight about myself and how I can develop myself further."
- "Interesting and a wake-up call for many other thoughts."
- "This program was very useful and informative."
- "Awesome education."
- "Healthy and will generate success."

Case History #3: A team working with Dynamic Value Congruence

This is a case study about a management team in a newly formed high school in Lund, Sweden. Two of the team members knew each other from previous work a long time ago but have not worked together in this type of setting. "Our management team is new, and we wanted a process that would help us get closer and become more effective together," says Malin, the principal of the school who initiated this process.

They all share the view that everyday life is demanding, and it can easily become a lot about doing and not much about reflection. They all agreed that they needed more reflection and discussions.

Through this process, they have found more opportunities for communication and have gotten to know each other on a deeper level. They are all different, and by doing this process, have achieved a deeper understanding of each other's needs.

Malin continues, "By giving us this time to go through this

process as a team, and the way the process is built up using the Dynamic Value Congruence tool, is a very good starting point for discussion. Instead of seeing differences, we now see similarities. As an example, we understand each other's perspectives and why this is important.

The process was quite redemptive for our team. Unfortunately, one of us is currently on sick leave, so nothing has turned out exactly as we had planned, but I think the work we did together also helped us to deal with our colleague's serious illness in a way that will bring our team even closer together in the long term.

I believe we were able to take some shortcuts in communication following our process. We now know a little more about how each member of the team thinks and what we value most. This makes it easier to overcome minor disagreements in everyday life. We've already opened the door to different perspectives. We have become even more secure together. We can talk about most things and give each other more personal space.

We were initially a little skeptical about using Zoom for part of the process, due to the pandemic, but were pleasantly surprised. Most things work just as well remotely as long as the technology works.

The result is that we found a route, a shortcut into speedier cooperation, which is crucial for our operating unit. We have become more effective in our communication. We all agree that there is a more confident and effective atmosphere shared by all in the management team.

The process for a team such as Hedda School could look like this:

This process can, as always, be adapted where necessary.

Dynamic value congruence process

Friday, May 29th 9:30 CTE	Monday, June 1st 9:45 CTE	Tuesday, June 2nd 9:45 CTE	Monday, June 8th 9:45 CTE	Tuesday, June 9th 9:45 CTE	TBD
Preparation Approx. 1 hour	**Module 1** 1-1.5 hours	**Module 2** 1 hour	**Module 3** 1-1.5 hours	**Module 4** 1 hours	**Module 5** 1-1.5 hours
Introduction to Values and Value Congruence	My Peronsal Journey	My Life Journey	Introduce myself to team	Developing Team Culture	Review and Recalibrate
• Explain Dynamic Value Congruence • Clarify Organisations Values - purpose, strategy, etc.	• Clarify personal values • Storytelling and Why • Values Track	• Share Event Journeys • Making connections between Values and Events in your Life Journey	• Self-presentation to team • Understanding Organisation's Values • What team culture is needed?	• What are our priority behaviours and practices to connect with organisation's purpose • Prepare to implement Plan	• What have we learned? • What has changed? • What do we need to do or change moving forward?
Complete Ind. Values Ranking	Prepare Event Journey	Prepare Self-Presentation	Complete Cultural Ranking	Implement Behavioural Plan	Carry on or Repeat Module 4

Case History #4: Individuals

Working with values on an individual basis is a great foundation for starting a coaching process. This consists of the basic process: three meetings during which the individual gains new insights and awareness of what drives them. These insights provide a compass for life, which can be put into action and supported with coaching. After ranking the values, followed by storytelling, the next steps can be used as best suits the individual.

The process of finding the stories around the values often generates an AHA moment, and incorporating these values into everyday life helps one becomes clearer, more credible, and more confident as an individual in both one's working and personal life. Reflection helps one to integrate the new learnings and identify new actions to explore through this development process. Here's how it helped Sara.

Sara's boss saw her potential as an employee but felt she needed more structure in her creativity and motivation. She wanted to help her avoid falling into her habitual traps and to give her a chance to thrive as an individual in her personal life, at work, and in her sport. So, she contacted me for help.

We started out with the basic process and followed up with regular coaching. All our meetings took place on Zoom. The result and learnings were amazing.

Sara has had therapy for years at different periods of her life. The values work and the meta-perspective she gained through reflection and the conversations in our sessions have helped her achieve fantastic success both in her personal life as well as at work. Not to mention winning a silver medal in the World Cup for juniors! That was a measurable result. The less obvious result was achieving lifelong knowledge and development as a human being, friend, and colleague.

The following is a summary of an exercise we call L.E.A.R.N. It describes lessons learned, using each letter of the word "learn," as described below.

L: Learn: I have gained knowledge about my personal values and an understanding of how the brain reacts to different levels of tension in the body—how my body reacts, for example, when I get nervous/stressed.

E: Enthusiasm: This is what I am most excited about. I am most happy to get confirmation through our conversation that I am heading in the right direction and can dare to continue on that path. Things have gotten clearer to me after mapping my values.

A: Add: This is what I want to know more about. I feel like I'm building my confidence every time we talk, and I'm understanding more and more about how my body reacts. But it's interesting to know how the brain works with the different hormones that kick in at different states, such as stress, fear, joy, etc.

R: Refocus: Fear: This is what worries me. I don't worry so much right now about the work I am doing with you and myself in particular.

N: Next step: This is what I will do. I will practice being in my calm and focused state of mind, especially now, before the World Cup, but also in other situations so that I don't have blackouts from stress and fear of failure.

Summary

Culture is the total sum of behavioural patterns, priorities, and values shared and communicated by the members of a particular group.
~Anthropologist Ralph Linton

Value.Online is a unique, interactive tool and not a test or an analysis.

By ranking what is most important to you right now, you gain insights and knowledge about yourself and your life. It can clarify whether you are living or not living your own personal values.

When a workgroup or organisation sets out to develop its common values and culture with the help of the Congruence Map, the common, normative values of the group will then guide the priorities and behaviours that are crucial to the success of the group's mission.

When working in a team with this process, it is important to provide support for the individual as well as for the team. The biggest takeaway is that the process helps to get people working together in a committed and motivated way—both in their personal lives and at work, where trust and conversation are the foundation.

If this also makes people more effective, clear, confident, and congruent, the potential possibilities for the future are unlimited. The dynamic of the Value tool is just as dynamic as we are as individuals.

Value.Online is available in thirteen languages and therefore works well in international and multilingual organisations. The participants are able to rank in their native language and then share their stories in the corporate language.

The tool and process are based on research and theories of consciousness and adult development described by: Milton Rokeach, Brian Hall, Abraham Maslow, and Shalom H. Schwartz, et al. We have 128 personal values that occur most commonly across the globe. Each value is given a definition using three synonyms. In this way, Value.Online is unique in that it covers almost four hundred values. Learn more at: https://www.value.se/en/value-online.

9

Trust is the Glue for Organization Change

By Patricia Dillon Saint

Change Leader | Coach | Author
Fishers, Indiana USA

"Trust is the glue that holds an organization together in the face of enormous challenges."

~Judith E. Glaser

Wake-Up Call

By mid-March 2020, paper towels were scarce on grocery store shelves, the United States National Basketball Association (NBA) terminated its season before the play-offs, and my two-week business trip to Switzerland was canceled.

The disruption to supply chains, professional spectator sports, and global travel was unprecedented and attributed to the growing threat of the COVID-19 virus. This storyline dominated newscasts about its unconfirmed origin and development of a vaccine during daily briefings among healthcare professionals, industry experts, and government officials. Ongoing communications by briefers and the media aimed to ease uncertainty and fear because, if left unchecked, it would fuel more confusion and distrust.

Simply stated, people wanted to know how this virus would affect their families, daily lives, and employment, yet no one could provide definitive answers during this initial period. It was unsettling yet the reality.

As uncertainty loomed, my youngest son moved temporarily from his downtown condo into our family home in a rural, lakeside community to quarantine and to work remotely. Within a day after his arrival, daily deliveries from Amazon became normal. I recall the first package delivered included one hundred StarKist™ tuna packs along with an assortment of granola bars. The next delivery was a multi-pack box with industrial paper towels, rubber bands, and staples to make homemade face masks until commercial ones were available. Those deliveries got my attention.

My son's insight was impressive. It sparked my realization that this virus would last much longer than a severe flu season and major change was underway—not only for individuals and families but also within organizations.

Embedding Organizational Change
Trust Instills Camaraderie

The initial concepts and disciplines of Organizational Change Management (OCM) surfaced in the early 1990s from well-known trailblazers that included: John Kotter (*Our Iceberg is Melting* in 1995) and Spencer Johnson (*Who Moved my Cheese?* in 1996).

Trust is a critical OCM component and intrinsic motivator for people to accept desired change. When people believe their leadership is trustworthy, it fuels a sense of psychological safety, a strong work culture, and camaraderie. If trust is low, resistance will most likely increase and jeopardize the outcomes of the change initiative.

As an organizational change leader and coach, I focus on developing strategies to transition people from their current state to the desired future state. The primary objective is to ensure *people are willing, ready, and able* to accept the desired change.

By applying deliberate change management processes, practices, and tools, it provides the OCM team with the means to:

- **analyze** the gap between the "As Is" and the "To Be" states
- **assess** stakeholder engagement to build trusted relationships
- **identify** risks, barriers, and impediments
- **develop** a strategic Change Plan and roadmap
- **plan** for continuous communication, learning, and coaching
- **measure** desired outcomes and success criteria

My appreciation for organizational change practices arose several years ago when I joined a lucrative start-up company that was disrupting the traditional aviation logistics industry. On my first day as employee number 26, I learned the company had been purchased by a Fortune 500 corporation, and my role had been expanded beyond marketing to operations and special projects. It was my first change initiative, and I didn't know enough to be scared!

The project was challenging because it entailed full-scale individual, organizational, and enterprise change. My ten-month strategic plan focused on three key objectives: relocate our employees and a multi-million-dollar aircraft parts inventory (housed in ten different locations) to a new corporate facility, oversee the system integration of bar code technology with our outdated financial management system, and support marketing and sales teams during client and customer visits at our new showroom facility. The leadership team was highly engaged, yet one seasoned stakeholder lagged initially in accepting the new inventory management system. It was an arduous journey that resulted in industry, corporate, and employee praise.

The most important take-away from this initiative remains steadfast in my change toolkit today. A well-designed plan is important, yet instilling trust in teams and building positive relationships at all levels (stakeholders, line managers, and employees) is critical for success because people naturally resist change.

Crisis Motivates People

In my experience, the most common barriers that often stall major organizational change initiatives are low trust in leadership, lack of purpose and desire, and over-complexity.

Undoubtedly, the global pandemic prompted organizations to plan, adapt, and work differently at lightning speed. The global scope and urgency to produce a global COVID-19 vaccine was emotional and personal for individuals, families, and organizations. It also defined a clear purpose. Given this scenario, initial resistance was most likely lower than normal in many organizations.

Despite challenges, organizations had to operate differently by:

- extending hours for essential personnel (as needed)
- establishing or expanding a remote workforce
- absorbing expenses for home office equipment and security software
- rethinking how to initiate or enhance communication channels remotely
- training people and teams to use communications tools (e.g., Zoom Video).
- canceling on-site workshops and retreats during lockdown periods
- learning to bond within teams and retain camaraderie in a virtual environment
- transforming toward a more agile organization and new ways of working
- adapting to desired behavioral change

Key Insights: Teams established and refined rules of engagement for virtual meetings that addressed: when to turn on/turn off the video (e.g., a 5 a.m. meeting without video is okay); when to schedule shorter, fifteen-minute check-ins; the importance of employee health and wellness; and when humor creates deeper team connection, such as if a child or dog appeared on a home office computer screen.

Tools Enable Change

Oftentimes, I rely on two of my favorite OCM assessment and process tools to determine the scope and scale of a new change initiative. Additionally, these tools aid in identifying the purpose, people, risk, resistance, complexity, and the change team resources needed to implement the change initiative.

If any of the tools are used, the findings provide insights to create a viable OCM strategy, plan, and team.

1: Change Curve	
Purpose	Assess the current state (denial, resistance, exploration, commitment) that resonates with an individual, group, or team about a change initiative.
Benefits	Gain awareness about the gap between the current state and future state of a change initiative. It should be done early and repeated to view progress with adjustments as needed.

How to Use	Identify the "State" on the Change Curve to assess the gap in moving toward the future state and to scale the scope, effort, and resources needed.
Definition of States and Leadership Engagement	
Denial	**People** realize change is not easy to accept and often react with shock.
	Leaders need to serve as role models to inform, communicate, and care throughout the change.
Resistance	**People** realize the change is happening and believe there is no way to avoid it.
	Leaders need to listen and empathize to minimize fears and distrust.
Exploration	**People and Teams** start learning new ways to constructively contribute toward the change yet have not fully accepted it.
	Leaders need to realize the acceptance is not finalized, yet encourage teams toward training, experimenting, knowledge sharing, and storytelling.

Commitment	**Teams** begin to feel more in control as they settle into their new roles; work activities return to normal.
	Leaders need to acknowledge and reward team members who are contributing and keep them motivated and committed.

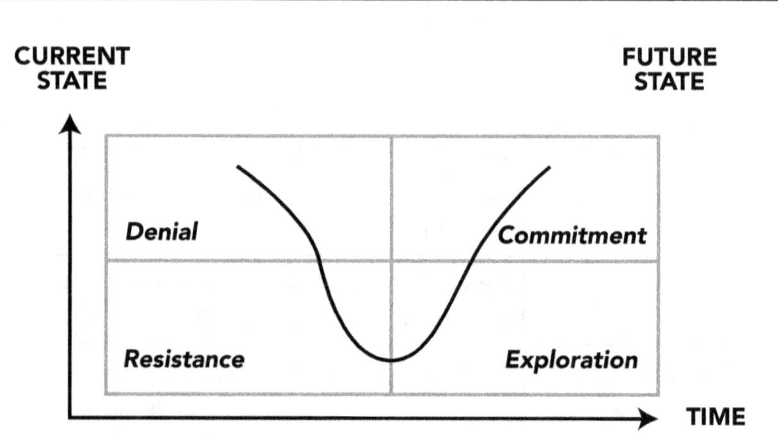

Source: Adapted from an earlier version of the source: Kübler-Ross (1969)

Key Insights

- OCM goal is to define and implement a strategy to accelerate adoption
- Recognize individuals experience change and transition differently
- Organizations apply OCM practices as a catalyst to collectively spark the desired change
- Ideally, the gap between the current and future state will decrease

2: Stakeholder Assessment on a Napkin	
Purpose	Assess Stakeholder Engagement and Buy-In for desired change
Benefits	The matrix distinguishes four quadrants with profiles and insights about how to engage each of the Stakeholder Groups: Advocates, Supporters, Critics, and Blockers. Typically, the change leaders will focus is on: • inspiring Advocates to serve as role models of change • identifying Blockers early to form a sponsor coalition of Advocates to influence the sentient of a Blocker to gain future endorsement • spending less time on influencing Supporters and Critics as they represent a lower risk to the change initiative **Source**: My adaptation of the Force Field Analysis first described by psychologist Kurt Lewin in the 1950s (Lewin, 1951).

How to Use	<ul><li>Conduct an informal assessment of key stakeholders by determining which profile best fits their current sentiment about the change initiative.</li><li>Identify any stakeholder that meets the Blocker profile.</li><li>Develop a plan to influence the Blocker (or remove as a last resort).</li><li>Limit formal documentation sharing, given the sensitivity.</li></ul>

Sustaining Organizational Change
Measuring Change

Indentify early
- Actively involve
- Find an influential advocate
- Win over via key opinion leader
- Potential Alligators

Avoid
- Bypass if feasible
- Typically not influential
- Engage with minimum effort

Blockers
Resistors are often difficult to persuade

Advocates
Positive Change Leaders

Typical Profiles

Critics
Negative yet pose minimal impact

Supporters
Will follow in time when ready

Indentify early
- Actively engage
- Praise their efforts often
- Leverage their influence
- Your Cheerleaders

Discover in Time
- Need more information
- Address concerns/ questions
- May sway in time - be patient

Measuring the impact of a desired change initiative is often overlooked yet critical in gaining acceptance and adoption. It also provides a pathway for continuous improvement.

The Change Leader should describe how to measure the results of the change initiative ideally in the Change Plan. The impact of the change can be measured using several techniques, primarily by conducting:

- change impact assessment tools
- periodic employee surveys that pose open questions

- interviews with stakeholders, teams, and individuals
- team coaching workshops to assess growth mindset and behavioral change

C-IQ Dashboard

As a coach certified in Conversational Intelligence®(C-IQ), one of my favorite assessments is the Conversational Dashboard™. Developed by Judith E. Glaser, it links the neuroscience behind trust with our words, conversations, and relationships. Judith's legacy lives deep within the C-IQ coaching community, and I am grateful for her lifelong work and passion.

The Conversational Dashboard™ is a simple, yet powerful assessment tool that identifies and describes five trust levels ranging from low to high, as cited:

Low Trust	Resistor and Skeptic
Conditional Trust	Wait and See
High Trust	"Experimenter" and Co-Creator

It can be applied with individuals and among teams and organizations. Ideally, it is best to conduct an initial assessment followed by periodic progress checks throughout the change initiative.

I have used this extensively with teams during role-play exercises by forming three groups:

- participants who play out scenarios of the trust levels
- coach who practices coaching skills to improve the trust level

- observers who collect and share feedback

Each group learns more about how words and conversations can affect trust in relationships. By embedding coaching practices (e.g., ask open questions, listen, and show empathy), the Conversational Dashboard™ provides a means to assess and strengthen trust.

To learn more about the C-IQ Dashboard™ and Trust Catalyst Tools®, visit the CreatingWe® Institute Website.[1]

Leaders as Coaches

The impact of COVID-19 is highlighting a need for strong leaders who can lead and instill trust despite chaos, crisis, and change.

According to *Forbes*, coaching is becoming a leadership development must at all levels of the organization. In the article, the author presents a case for investing in coaching as a leadership development: *"Why is coaching so critical to career advancement? Because it's not just about professional development, but about boosting your employees' confidence and building strong communication skills, thus improving their performance and productivity."*[2]

Unlike consulting firms that provide experts who advise and tell senior leaders how to implement the desired change—coaching offers a unique approach that centers on mutual trust, goal setting, action plans, and sustaining long-term results.

Today, successful organizational change depends on effective leaders who have strong communication skills, agility, and empathy. Additionally, leaders must instill trust within their organizations since the rate of change and process improvement is not waning. For this reason, coaching is a perfect partnership with organizational change.

> When we tell people to do their jobs, we get workers.
> When we trust people to get the job done, we get leaders.
> —Simon Sinek

Endnotes:

1. The Prosci ADKAR® Model, Prosci, Inc. https://www.prosci.com/methodology/adkar.
2. Dweck C.S. (2006). Mindset: The New Psychology of Success, New York: Ballantine Books.
3. Glaser J. E. (2014). Conversational Intelligence: How Great Leaders Build Trust and Get Extraordinary Results, New York: Bibliomotion, Inc.
4. CreatingWe® Institute, https://conversationalintelligence.com/services/catalyst-tools.
5. "Why Leaders Should Consider Shifting to Coaching Leadership Style Now More Than Ever," Kara Dennison, Forbes, https://www.forbes.com/sites/karadennison/2021/09/20/why-leaders-should-consider-shifting-to-a-coaching-leadership-style-now-more-than-ever/?sh=64d738362f81, Sep 20, 2021.

10

Smart Future Workplaces: Realistic Solutions for Tough Business Environments

By Ute Franzen-Waschke

Coaching Across Hierarchies | Facilitation
Workshop & Program Design
Holle, Germany

The year 2020 was far from ordinary. It may have started for most of us quite normally but quickly turned into something nobody could have predicted. In my personal situation, the year did have the potential to turn into something not-so-ordinary—but not necessarily for the reasons you might think. My husband was sent abroad on an international assignment by his employer, and I was going to join him. Our idea had been to enjoy the time abroad by traveling across the US, visiting friends, and exploring a few corners of the country that we hadn't visited. I was also looking forward to seeing my American and Canadian colleagues and friends, who wouldn't be too far from where we would be based in the US.

Aspirations, joyful anticipation, and concrete plans—our adventure was ready to begin…and then it all came out so differently. When we touched down in the US on March 3, 2020, the pandemic was already underway. Yet most of us were hoping that with spring coming, the worst could be prevented, and the spread of the virus could be contained.

Well, we all know that things ended differently and that we now can see some light at the end of the tunnel. But who knows what working life and life in general will look like once we follow that shimmer of light and exit that tunnel? Back in March 2020, my husband and I managed to get the most important household appliances for our apartment in the US before the lockdown began. Then his assignment began, and he spent nearly the entire time working from our apartment—what we called our home at that time, and not with his colleagues on premises somewhere in Michigan. For me, it wasn't any different. Because my clients were located in Europe and Germany, it had been clear, even before the extent and the impact of the pandemic were known, that I would be mainly working from the apartment in Rochester, Michigan, serving my clients in Europe, and later on, new clients in Canada and the US.

Before I boarded the plane with my husband, some of my clients had already agreed to continue to work with me using the video conferencing tool Zoom, which I had been using for some years with my international clients and the global coach communities I am involved in. For my clients, such remote communication was anything but normal back in March 2020, but they were curious and trusting enough to try. After a few weeks, all my clients in Germany and Europe were in the same situation as me.

Due to the pandemic and precautionary measures to control the spread of the virus, all of a sudden, *everyone* had to work from their homes. And just like that, it wasn't anything special anymore. This "working from home thing" had gone viral. Operating from home and connecting with colleagues, customers and clients, and external service providers, such as me, using digital technologies, had turned out to be the only way to stay in touch and remain in business. And that was when a new era began.

We were all right there, witnessing the moment, but when we were in it, we couldn't know how much of a paradigm shift it would really become, for companies, businesses, my clients, the coaching profession, myself, and everyone else on this planet.

History

Let's rewind the story of my clients by a few more years and take a look at what working at home meant for them before the pandemic hit in 2020. Working from home was a privilege for most, a privilege that came with positions, job descriptions, and the mindsets of the respective bosses. Though data had long shown that working from home did indeed have positive implications for job satisfaction, performance, and talent retention, it wasn't anything a company would necessarily offer to *every* staff member.

In May 2020, I wrote an article for the Forbes Coach Council about the hurdles many of my clients had to overcome to become part of that privileged group of employees entitled to work from home from time to time, or as agreed in advance with their supervisors. They had to patiently wait their turn to be granted that privilege, even though they were usually unclear as to what factors actually decided when their turn would come. Depending on the bosses, they might have had to demonstrate particular traits in the workplace, e.g., demonstrate trustworthiness, taking away the fears and concerns of those supervisors that when they were "out of sight," or working from home, they would still be "good employees" and not cheat on the company by actually taking care of private chores rather than working on their job tasks.

The article provides you with more details, also referencing studies available a long time before the pandemic, speaking to this non-transparent world of working from home and the mystery and obstacles of being admitted to this circle of "worthy and good" employees who were granted the privilege of working from home.

With the pandemic threatening the economic survival of so many organizations, necessity became once again the mother of invention back in 2020, when suddenly—because companies wouldn't have survived any other way—basically everyone was allowed to work from home. This came as a surprise to the majority of the population, and because it happened basically overnight, neither organizations nor the workforce was prepared. Only those who already enjoyed this "remote" privilege could adapt quickly to these new necessities, at least from a technical point of view.

Everyone else was struggling not just because of the new situation at the workplace, which was now in their living rooms, dining rooms, and at kitchen tables, but also because it was not just the workplace of *one* family member but of *all* the members who either had a job to do from home or who had gone to school or university before and were now home-schooled.

That added a much higher level of difficulty to this already unfamiliar situation. Not just one area, but an entire system started to change. With what we know now we are only starting to grasp the complexity of the situation, which had come down on organizations, employees, families, and communities overnight. With the huge learnings made about what's possible and the desires this unleashed in companies, businesses, and employees alike, we are now moving toward something whose gestalt we cannot fully see and recognize—not quite yet.

Employees mastered the unthinkable. They worked effectively and productively from home, and with that, gained a new confidence and desire regarding how to take more control over and shape their working lives differently going forward. How would organizations be able to turn back the clock—if they even wanted to—to times before the pandemic?

Opportunities have opened for organizations in the same way they opened up for employees. There will be interesting times ahead, times that will require a structured approach to deconstruct the complexities and pluralities of needs and interests with the multitude of stakeholders. Meet the PPAS

Maturity Model®—a model that has been applied and tested and is simple enough to help coaches, leaders, and anyone else going through change and longing for clarity and structure in times of ambiguity, chaos, and confusion.

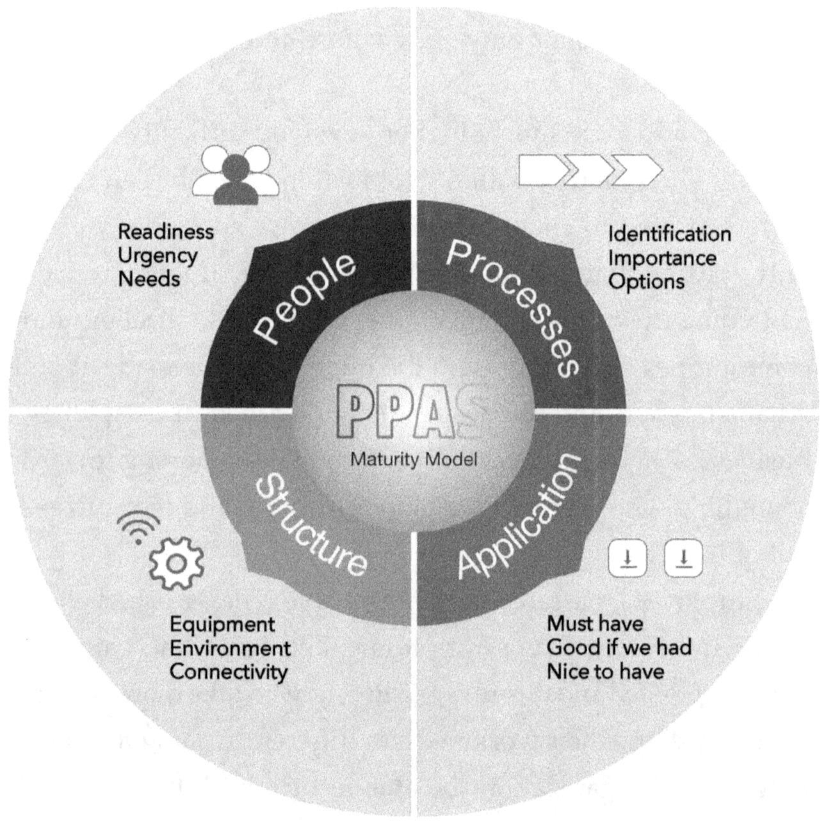

Discover - Analyze - Succeed

Discover how the model, whose popularity peaked during the pandemic, continues to provide valuable guidance as organizations and employees are working to find their ways back into "normal" work situations. However, nothing seems normal anymore. With their experiences during the pandemic and their newly gained confidence, the workforce is re-entering the workspace with a different picture of what they would like their working lives to be.

Similarly, companies and businesses have seen new possibilities; for example, talent can be located anywhere and is not limited to headquarters or physical locations they have around the globe. With that could come huge savings on real estate as well as payroll. These are just a few aspects in a myriad, depending on industries and geographies.

The PPAS Maturity Model® was used in a more covert manner before the pandemic, when I was coaching my one-on-one clients and teams. I was using it more for my own sake as a coach to make sense of what I was hearing, to help clarify complex stories and situations my clients were bringing to the sessions. I was also using it to help my clients discover and uncover aspects they hadn't yet seen and that would help them to see clearer as well and envision which next steps they could consider and eventually take. In 2020, during the pandemic, the model was used more explicitly and overtly in helping individuals and organizations make sense in a structured, yet flexible manner to work through the transitions and changes that they were all experiencing in real-time and on the fly.

As organizations and individuals are slowly moving out of the pandemic and back into their offices and working lives—be it (fully) remote, hybrid, or whatever name is given to the workplace of the future in the respective eco-systems of various industries and business sectors—the PPAS Maturity Model® is maturing in itself and in the diverse contexts it has been applied to so far.

The present and the future

A user's guide was written and published in April 2021 on how to best use the PPAS Maturity Model® to create successful remote work cultures. The avatars, Jenn, Laura, and Cynthia, who accompanied the readers through the model and its dimensions in the user's guide, were also featured in the Forbes Coach Council in a sequel, within which they described their personal reflections about where the corporate world is headed now that the pandemic has slowed down a bit and vaccination rates are on the rise.

Here is a story about one of my book avatars, Jenn.

Jenn's mission is to do the seemingly impossible: to come up with a strategy on what the future of work could look like in her organization. Jenn is a senior-level executive at an automotive company and has been with the company for more than ten years. In her mission, Jenn needs to tackle some serious decisions with her senior leadership team, namely, how to best lay the foundation for a workplace of the future that is attractive for the biggest assets of the company—their people—while remaining competitive and innovative for their customers in a very tough industry, which was already going through some rough times before the pandemic added its special twist.

This begged the questions: How was she to juggle all the different expectations from their workforce that she and her team had learned about in a survey they conducted at the beginning of 2021? How could the workforce remain productive, efficient, and customer-centric while spread not just across the globe in different physical company locations but also now across different physical households: home offices, offices, co-working spaces, and basically anyplace else with an internet connection?

On the one side, COVID-19 set strict boundaries for people in terms of their freedom to move about, and on the other, COVID-19 also removed boundaries dramatically in terms of people's freedom from where to work, particularly in so-called knowledge worker positions. However, Jenn's company is operating in an industry where there are not just knowledge workers. It's hardware, it's logistics, it's production, and so many more functions that are simply not made for these new concepts, at least not at first sight or on a long-term basis.

To tackle the task, Jenn invited a coach to work with her team, hoping that clarity would emerge for the complexity of the mission that she saw ahead. The project with the coach was kicked-off with a workshop in which the focus was primarily on getting a general overview of what needs had come out of the company employee survey and then which of those needs could be acknowledged and accommodated immediately and which would have to be put on the backburner for the time being.

To determine how to proceed, more questions needed to be addressed, such as: Where were overlaps of needs or synergies in what the workforce would like to see and what the company would be prepared to offer moving toward "the place one would want to work in the future"? Where might there be gaps that needed to be addressed within the workforce in the next few months to co-create a strategy, or maybe different strategies, of what these future workplaces could look like for Jenn's organization or for at least certain parts of it? The varying needs they found from their business units, functions, departments, and individuals might not allow for a feasible one-size-fits-all strategy.

Jenn had already thought a lot about the situation her company was in—the opportunities that had come with the new situation, and equally, the threats. She realized that awareness of the situation, allowing for pluralities instead of creating unified standards, and a one-way approach to this dilemma would be a great realization for the senior leadership team to walk away with and make peace with.

This awareness helped them realize that letting go of their desire to fix this in a general and standardized way—as they were used to doing—and instead allowing conversations to take place at the various levels in the organization to create some guiding principles, frameworks, and models would help them explore which scenarios would work where rather than trying to find *the one solution* for the *entire* organization that is so often rolled out from the top to the operating and working levels.

For a senior leadership team, it takes a lot to let go of these known and trusted principles, especially in difficult times when there are already so many uncertainties. Often, their go-to is to increase control and not release it. To be open to influence without a fixed agenda is already challenging in less-threatening situations, and yet it is a wonderful vantage point, too, when exploring especially unknown and unchartered territory.

That's exactly what Jenn, her senior leadership team, and the coach were about to embark on: a journey of which the outcome was open and couldn't be boxed just after a one-day workshop. Jenn admitted that she felt a tad uneasy as she didn't want to waste the time of the senior leadership team. Yet she realized they had to start somewhere, and that somewhere was today and with the approach Jenn and her coach had worked out together.

Jenn had been involved in the preparation of the workshop, and therefore, she wasn't as surprised as her colleagues were about the opening questions the coach asked at the start of their joint journey:

1. From a work point of view: What did you learn about yourself last year when you were working fully from home? What would you like to keep, maintain, and not change back? And what did you miss during the pandemic? What would you like to claim back and do more of again now that it seems possible again?
2. What would a smart future workplace look like for you?

The leadership team worked in dyads and triads to explore these questions. They started off with the first set of questions.

Some said they had missed the connection and social interaction in the office. Others highlighted the need to work while focused and uninterrupted. The extra time they had won by not having to commute or go on business trips were highlighted as benefits some had learned to appreciate and wouldn't want to give up anymore—or at least, they didn't want to go back 100 percent to what their working lives were like before. It's not always fun to be a frequent traveler and world traveler for the company. More quality time with family members, many realized, wasn't too bad either. The new dimensions of their relationships with colleagues in the workplace were also mentioned.

This more complete picture of our colleagues, which included these glimpses into their family situations and homes, all of which felt a bit odd and inappropriate in the beginning, in retrospective, allowed for a much better understanding of the employee as a whole person as opposed to just the employee one normally sees at work. Those were just a few things voiced in those first conversations around the first set of questions.

Jenn was convinced that what the leadership team had reflected on, mentioned, and brought up in their conversations was now more conscious and present for them. This would equip them well for the decisions ahead in the dimension of "People," as well as regarding the jobs and tasks people perform at work and the roles both play, the needs that come with these, and how these needs play out in different future workplace scenarios.

"People" who are more extraverted, who are inspired by the chatter and noise in the office and by the ability to bounce off ideas with a real person just across their cubicle walls, differ from those who are more introverted and prefer to work quietly and focused and only share thoughts and opinions when they are mentally ready and prepared to do so. The privacy of their homes would perhaps allow for that to happen in a better way than in an open-plan office—depending, of course, on household composition and living situations when working from home.

As a next step, the coach asked Jenn and her senior leadership team a few questions from a questionnaire she had prepared based on research work Nancy P. Rothbard had done. Rothbard studies people in the workplace and how they draw boundaries between their personal and professional lives as well as the role technology plays.

Before the pandemic:

- Did you keep your private time strictly private and your work time strictly for matters at work?
- Did you socialize with colleagues after work/outside work?
- Did you use the flexible working models your company offers?
- Did you work at fixed times even though your employer offers you some flexibility?
- Hot-desking is a concept I have issues with.
- I can work from anywhere—no problem.

Some of the questions and statements do not necessarily

fit the working conditions of members of the senior leadership team, but they helped again to broaden their perspectives and raise awareness for the decisions they would possibly be making, not just for themselves but for their workforce in general. Hot-desking, for example, is a concept in which staff does not have a personal desk. Instead, the desk is shared among colleagues at different times of the day or different days of the week. Such a concept might not apply to a CEO, and yet, the C-Suite or executive levels decide on these principles to save real estate costs and reduce office space. Yes, CEOs are very used to working from anywhere, but some people on other working levels might not have that experience, preference, and flexibility. Stepping into the shoes of those for whom we are making decisions can be an eye-opening exercise and a good warm-up for such a journey.

That's what Jenn thought too. The coach had briefed Jenn before the workshop that the questions she was going to ask the leadership team about these flexible working models would point to research done by Nancy P. Rothbard. Rothbard's research showed that some employees would more favor a stricter separation between their working lives and their private lives than others. She called them "segmentors" and "integrators."

This preference would show up, for example, in a separation between "Time and Space" and with whom workers socialize with in their free time. Segmentors would keep business and private fairly separate, whereas integrators would mix and merge as they see fit and as works best for them.

Separate work phones, calendars, and places where "work" would happen on the one side, and on the other, one smartphone, one calendar, and "work" happens where it's the most convenient, not necessarily in an office.

Why would that be important? Because during the heavy

Time & Space

Calendar

- Separate or combined
- Mixing events or not
- Take odd-time calls from office or home

Space

- Hot-desking/desk sharing
- Family visits on premises
- Separate room at home to work from or 'in the living room'

Me

- Dress code similar or different when working from home
- Socializing with colleagues outside of working time
- Use on-site services such as dry cleaning, child care etc..

working-from-home periods, segmentors, in particular, had to get their heads around how to still separate work from their private lives when work moved in with them at home. Not an easy task. This is a situation that most segmentors would like to reverse again as soon as possible as they long to get back the stricter and easier separation between the two worlds.

Therefore, basing a decision from where to work solely on an individual's—a CEO's or senior leadership team's point of view—bears some pitfalls. There are far more factettes to that decision and often underlying psychological patterns and needs that the individual can't even name but that make them "feel better" or "feel worse" at work. The notion of "feeling good" was something that suffered during the pandemic as well. Jenn knew that.

Many conversations she had with people in the company confirmed that the data collected in 2020 was right: Well-being and engagement ranked high on the list of states to be restored again among the workforce—and at her workplace. Hence, when shaping the workplace of the future, she felt that attention should be paid to what favors well-being and engagement in the company and what doesn't. Being aware and acknowledging such little things as whether I am asking a segmentor or an integrator to enjoy the pleasures of hot-desking, which could either foster or suppress their well-being, is an important factor. That was now clear to her *and* to the members of the senior leadership team, thanks to the intervention with the coach during the workshop.

Before Jenn and her team set off to discover the second question about what a smart future workplace scenario would look like for them, the coach invited all of them to consider the adjective *smart* and the acronym *SMART*. Both are omnipresent in our world. We have smartwatches, smartphones, smart TVs, and smart refrigerators. Every worker in the company knows what SMART goals are. So, what have these smart devices and the acronym SMART got to do with creating smart future workplace scenarios? The coach didn't come unprepared and invited Jenn and her team to listen and reflect on what—from the coach's point of view—the acronym SMART meant in connection with future workplace scenarios. Future workplace scenarios should be:

S: Sensible

M: Motivating

A: Agreed

R: Realistic & Resource-Oriented

T: Time-Limited

The coach explained that future work is **SMART** when it is planned in a **SENSIBLE** way. What does that mean? It must make sense from a company perspective *and* from an employee perspective. If the company tries to meet the wishes and needs of their workforce so badly that they cannot do their core business anymore at their best (in their most effective and efficient way), the company will not be able to survive economically and will disappear from the business landscape soon. In the same way as when the company is not making enough use of SENSIBLE ways to maximize new opportunities that have come with the pandemic and because of the pandemic to offer people autonomy and flexibility so they can work at their best.

Future work is **SMART** when it is **MOTIVATING.** What motivates the individual and the team is something that needs to be discovered and explored. It's not the same for every one of us but very worthwhile to be clear about because with increased motivation, engagement levels rise, and with it, so do productivity levels and output or outcomes for the company and the employees. People feel good when they accomplish things, when there is meaning and purpose in what they do, and research proves that this has positive effects on business' bottom lines.

Future work is SMART when it's **AGREED.** That means when individuals do not decide purely based on their own needs and what is best for them but co-create and agree on rules of engagement: ways and days of working with those "human interfaces" in the workplace with whom they are trying to get a project through the door: colleagues, customers, and clients.

Future work is SMART when it's **REALISTIC** and **RESOURCE-ORIENTED.** A company can't offer jobs that require certain equipment, such as test benches, machinery, and any other expensive stuff that needs to be dragged into the office for two days and then taken back home again for the rest of the working week. A company also cannot have the equipment available in both places, the office and at home, as this would be too expensive. We are not speaking about laptops here but hi-tech and often customized technical equipment in the six-digit sphere. Hence, when it is unrealistic for some types of jobs to work from home in a flexible manner, it's good to acknowledge and accept this; such a mindset can help when one must look for other possibilities on how to allow flexibility and autonomy also in those areas of work.

Future work is SMART when it's **TIME-LIMITED.** Nothing lasts forever, not even love, so why would one think that working arrangements have an extended shelf life? Especially, in those fast-paced, VUCA (stands for Volatility, Uncertainty, Complexity, and Ambiguity and describes work environments that often change and therefore require adaptation and flexibility by leaders and staff) environments, and agile work environments, one must regularly revisit arrangements and agreements and see whether they are still serving us in the best possible manner. That applies as well to what a team or a business decides in the moment about what SMART Future Work means for them. It's a snapshot in the context of the here and now. And the snapshot might look different in the future and therefore needs regular updates and check-ups. The coach's perspectives and insights about SMART future workplace scenarios equipped the senior leadership team for the next round of conversations on that workshop day. Jenn and her team would explore "The PPAS Maturity Model®" and its four dimensions. Jenn had arranged for a live and in-person setting. The coach would use floor and desk mats to make participants of the workshop "step into" each dimension. For virtual workshops, the coach had shown Jenn the Miro Boards and Howspace workspaces that were prepared and used to support a virtual experience around the four dimensions of the model:

People
Processes
Applications
Structure

Even though Jenn and her team had arranged for an in-person experience, Jenn had already spoken with her coach on how to scale these types of workshops across the entire organization over the next six or twelve months. Then virtual settings could be more suitable, depending on group size, locations, and budgets available. That would be no problem, as last year, the coach had used the PPAS Maturity Model already and solely in virtual settings. During the in-person workshop, Jenn and her team were invited to embark on a World Café tour to explore each dimension of the PPAS Maturity Model, always in view of the elements that shape SMART future workplace scenarios.

Jenn and her colleagues were familiar with the World Café method in which World Café Travelers move from table to table and add to the conversations that had taken place there before. One table host stays at the table the entire time to provide background and details about previous conversations held on the respective topics. For the PPAS Maturity Model, there was one table per dimension. In a virtual meeting, the coach had explained there would be one topic per Zoom or MS Teams breakout room, and findings would be collected with the SuperChat widget on Howspace, a virtual collaboration platform the coach had used for some time already for such online or even hybrid versions of the workshop.
Jenn and her team explored the following questions at the different World Café stations:

People:

- What do I personally need to feel engaged and motivated in this new workplace scenario?
- How do my personal needs fit with the needs and requirements of the organization, the team, and our customers?

- How can we integrate the I inside the WE?—Autonomy versus Community/Organization?

Processes:

- Which processes in the workplace do we have?
- How do we need to adapt them to make them fit future workplace scenarios? For example, onboarding and offboarding processes in the organization? Performance reviews and career development?
- How can we ensure that also those who are not that often in the office are and feel included and are and feel seen regarding their accomplishments and contributions?

Applications:

- Which tools are we using in the organization?
- How well do they serve our needs?
- How tool-savvy are we/is our workforce?
- Are we only adding tools but not replacing any? How can we "clean up" the tool landscape?

Structure:

- How compatible are my personal "structures" with the team structures?
- How well can I work from home?
- Which tasks can I perform better at home/in the office? How can that be reflected in my work schedule?
- What impact does this have on my team/colleagues and customers?

- How much transparency can I apply in discussing these structural implications with them?

Where possible, Jenn and her team were also encouraged by the coach to determine some high-level aspects to further explore in the workshops that were already planned going forward, allowing a deeper dive into each dimension, also mixing the teams with next-level leaders to slowly but steadily involve the entire organization more into the process of shaping the future of work at Jenn's employer. At the workshop, it had become clearer to Jenn and the team that the whole company was in the midst of this process, and they had become aware that they would have to re-adjust and re-visit these topics again and again, iteration after iteration, to ensure the most recent developments in the world—health and business-wise—are reflected in what would be best for the employer and employee going forward.

After the first workshop, Jenn was content that she and her team were leaving with three MVPs (Minimal Viable Products) to further experiment and to test with their next-level leadership team. They decided on other learning, application, and adaptation loops that would follow. Smart future work is time-limited and only a snapshot solution for a particular period, no more and no less.

That was now crystal-clear to Jenn and her team. Agility and VUCA in action. Jenn was wondering how difficult or easy it would be for leaders in the company to embrace the fact that solutions for future workplace scenarios would be time-limited and diverse. Something that she would soon learn much more about when similar journeys would be kicked off throughout the entire organization.

How is your organization coping and managing the aspects of smart future workplace scenarios?

Resources:

"On the Precipice of a Culture Shift, Adaptation May Come at Warp Speed," Franzen-Waschke, U. (2020). Forbes Coach Council https://www.forbes.com/sites/forbescoachescouncil/2020/05/19/on-the-precipice-of-a-culture-shift-adaptation-may-come-at-warp-speed.

"Where Is The Corporate World Headed After The Pandemic? The Answer Is Complex," Franzen-Waschke, U. (2021). Forbes Coach Council: https://www.forbes.com/sites/forbescoachescouncil/2021/07/26/where-is-the-corporate-world-headed-after-the-pandemic-the-answer-is-complex.

Litchfield, P., Cooper, C., Hancock, C., Watt, P. (2016). "Work and Wellbeing in the 21st Century," International Journal of Environmental Public Health, 13(11), 1065, https://doi.org/10.3390/ijerph13111065.

Rothbard, N.P. (2020). "Building Work-Life Boundaries in the WFH Era," Harvard Business Review, REPRINT H05QN5, https://hbr.org/2020/07/building-work-life-boundaries-in-the-wfh-era.

"World Café Method," The World Café, http://www.the-worldcafe.com/key-concepts-resources/world-cafe-method.

"Minimum Viable Products," Wikipedia, December 10, 2021, https://en.wikipedia.org/wiki/Minimum_viable_product.

About the Authors

Christian Délez

https://ch.linkedin.com/in/christiandelez

Areas of Expertise:
Agile Project Leader | Coach | Facilitator

Christian Délez is passionate about team dynamics and culture design. Christian works in a big Swiss company (RUAG), where he implements the future of work patterns for more wholeness, purpose, and high performance. He loves trying new human interaction patterns to bring happiness to each individual in families, relationships, and at work. Christian is a co-founder of the Greatness Guild, the Swiss Association for Responsive Organisations and Good Practice Group. Christian works as deputy development manager at RUAG AG and has over twenty years of project and agile work experience in healthcare, telecommunications, and defense.

Ute Franzen-Waschke, MA (WBIS), PCC

http://www.discover-your-choices.de/en/coach

Areas of Expertise:
Coaching across hierarchies | Virtual & f2f Facilitation, Workshop & Program Design

Ute holds a master's degree in coaching and international business communication (WBIS). She works with individuals and teams on communication processes, relationship building, and co-creating work environments for individuals and teams to thrive. Ute's clients span the automotive and insurance industries as well as the public sector and start-ups. Ute also provides training for coaches in different coach certification programs, is a mentor listed in the ICF Mentor Coach Directory, and is a senior consultant at the CreatingWE Institute. Before Ute started her own business, she worked in multinationals in various roles for more than fifteen years.

Deborah Goldstein, ACC

deb@DRIVENpros.com www.DRIVENpros.com

Areas of Expertise:
Cultural transformation | Women's leadership |
JEDI (Justice, Equity, Diversity, Inclusion)

As a coach, facilitator, and consultant, Deborah works with NY, the US, and international organizations and individuals who are motivated to thrive in the twenty-first-century workplace environment. She focuses on two essential areas: creating psychological safety in the workplace and DRIVEN's signature programming in Intentional Productivity—which allows for thoughtful efficiency at work and space for wellness and focus in order to appreciate a full presence in life. Deborah considers herself to be DRIVEN's best student, embracing a fluid work-life rhythm that allows for continual growth and gratitude.

Varda Trauger Kauffmann

https://ANIOUway.com

Areas of Expertise:
Executive coaching | Team coaching
Embodied and Mindful Leadership | Facilitator| Speaker

The quest to find the right balance between the need to belong and to contribute, as well as her drive to stay true to herself, led Varda to develop ANIOU™: how WE include, respect, and support each other as distinct unique individuals and connect into healthy, resilient, and thriving organizations, businesses, and communities. Varda's journey as an RD manager in the non-profit sector inspired her to embrace her passion for people. Certified as a coach since 2008, she helps leaders and their teams to grow and achieve their goals, individually and as teams in the ANIOU™ way.

Linda Keller

lk@lk-lingo.com

Areas of Expertise:
Leadership and Team Development | Transition Coaching
Cross-Cultural Business Communication | Life coaching

Linda's passion is enabling individuals and teams to unleash their full potential by becoming more self-aware of who they are and how they communicate and by mastering their relationships with others. When people communicate effectively, they not only achieve incredible results but also do so more quickly, have fun, build trust, and become more resilient. Her clients span the global automotive, IT, pharmaceutical, insurance, and banking industries as well as public administration and higher education across Germany, the UK, China, Sweden, and Croatia. She holds several coaching certifications, including Conversational Intelligence®, and is a university lecturer for intercultural communication and English.

Karin Ovari

https://karinovari.com
https://www.linkedin.com/in/karinovari

Areas of Expertise:
Behavioural Safety Leadership &
Team Coaching & Development
Designer for the Future of Human Connection

 Karin brings thirty-plus years' leadership experience in various-sized organisations and across multiple disciplines, from co-leading expeditions in Antarctica working on oil rigs to training in the corporate IT world.

As a global citizen living on her fifth continent, and known as "the Aussie" in Scotland, she comes with a broad and deep understanding of people, behaviours, cultures, and communication styles. Her coaching studies bring a lifetime of practice and theory to life.

Patricia Dillon Saint

https://www.linkedin.com/in/patricia-saint-0b9b5a19

Areas of Expertise:
Change Leader, Coach, and Author

As a Change Leader and Coach, Pat has a wealth of business experience in organizational transformation, Information Technology (IT) consulting, and supply chain operations with Fortune 500 companies—primarily in healthcare, aviation, and military defense-regulated industries She is a Certified Coach in Conversational Intelligence® (C-IQ); a Certified Master Coach; and a Certified Prosci™ Change Management Practitioner and embeds team-coaching practices to spark positive change.

Pat is an author and has been a speaker at CAMP IT conferences and local chapters of the Project Management Institute (PMI) and the Association of Change Management Professionals (ACMP).

Carina Vinberg, PCC

https://www.linkedin.com/in/carina-vinberg-943aa440
https://framgangare.se/en/home

Areas of Expertise:
Leadership training | Value driven processes for higher trust
Virtual & F2F facilitation

Generous, curious, and engaged, Carina has enormous energy and a strong focus. Her passion lies in helping clients identify their values and core competencies so they become clearer and more confident and credible as individuals and leaders. Taking a neuroscience-based approach, she contributes to trusting cultures with greater well-being and better cooperation and achievement. Carina triggers growth, innovation, awareness, and practice through tools for successful self-leadership. With fifteen-plus years of experience as a self-employed coach, she has worked with executives and top athletes. Her clients span the sectors of investment, IT, start-up, insurance, and education at sports academies. Carina holds multiple coaching certifications.

Charlotte Weston-Horsmann

linkedin.com/in/charlotte-weston-horsmann-pcc-7b618349

Areas of Expertise:
Executive Coaching
Intercultural Communication Competence
TeamCoaching | Leadership Development

With over fifteen years of experience as an external coach in global organizations, Charlotte helps international professionals communicate effectively across cultures and develop leadership skills and situational communication agility. As a project manager in the non-profit sector with project sites situated in North Africa and the Middle East, she was instrumental in aligning international partners, project teams, and USAID toward a common purpose. After her ICF certification, Charlotte shifted her focus to working with international executives and clinical study project teams in the pharmaceutical sector to coordinate collaboration. As a result of cocreative coaching partnerships, we continue to create team cultures of inclusivity.

Catharina Wöhlecke-Haglund

linkedin.com/in/catharina-wöhlecke-haglund

Areas of Expertise:
Leadership trainer | Coach | Change facilitator

Catharina's diverse experience and background have helped her develop a coaching style that works. She has an extensive toolbox for leadership and team development, to be used when needed, with exercises, theory, templates, and follow-up tools. She has worked with airlines, banks, insurance, hospitals, government agencies, and many other industries. By designing processes, programs, and activities, Catharina helps people, teams, and organizations to help themselves. Changing culture, teambuilding, leadership, communication, resolving conflicts, and reaching outside of the comfort zone, Catharina brings a mix of warm support and sharp challenge to the table. Flipped classroom online training is her latest development.